WE REACH
THE MOON

WE REACH THE MOON

Young Readers' Edition Revised

A *New York Times* Book
by JOHN NOBLE WILFORD

Based upon the original book published by
𝕿𝖍𝖊 𝕹𝖊𝖜 𝖄𝖔𝖗𝖐 𝕿𝖎𝖒𝖊𝖘 *and Bantam Books*

A THISTLE BOOK
Published by
GROSSET & DUNLAP, INC.
A National General Company
New York

To Nona and Susan

Photographs courtesy of NASA

3173

Acknowledgments

This is, first and foremost, a newspaper reporter's book. I am not a scientist or engineer. But my years of covering the Apollo Project were an enlightening adult-education course in the fields of knowledge I either neglected as a university student or was not even exposed to in the pre-space curriculum. Nor am I a certified historian. But no journalist who looks beyond his typewriter can ignore the elements of history in the raw material that is his story.

And I am not—I was about to say, I am not a romantic, a dreamer, for journalists pride themselves on being detached observers of other men's passions. But who could cover the story of man's first footsteps on another world, and cover it as more than science story or another nuts-and-bolts technology story, without feeling in himself a flutter of all the romantic urges that have sent men across oceans, up mountains, and out into the air and then the space beyond the air? I could not.

Whatever future historians may say of Apollo, I will be grateful to *The New York Times* for the opportunity to be a close observer of this great adventure.

74 8830

This is not solely my book. I owe a large debt to a number of members of the *Times* staff, including Walter Sullivan, Henry R. Lieberman, Richard Witkin, Harold M. Schmeck, Jr., Sandra Blakeslee, and Douglas Kneeland. Their stories and editorial assistance were an invaluable contribution to the book. The diagrams are the work of the *Times* map department, headed by Andrew Sabbatini.

I want to single out for credit Richard D. Lyons, a boon companion and especially helpful colleague through all the major Apollo missions, and William K. Stevens, who provided most of the material and writing for the chapter on the Apollo 11 crew. Another good companion and colleague through all this was Douglas M. Dederer, who was especially helpful during my many visits to Cape Kennedy. The National Aeronautics and Space Administration and many of the major Apollo industrial contractors helped make available the many documents and background materials that facilitated coverage of Apollo.

Others who made the book possible were Carter Horsley and Sydnor Vanderschmidt, who made important research contributions. Mark Bloom was kind enough to read and offer suggestions on a part of the book. Mary Rourke typed much of the manuscript.

No one gave me more encouragement than my wife, Nancy, who shares my enthusiasm for the story and was uncomplaining of the time taken from our lives by the program to get men to the moon.

Every writer needs an editor, and I was fortunate to have two very skillful and understanding editors—Lee Foster and Donald Johnston. Michael A. Chester was the able editor of this particular edition of the book. Finally, I want to thank Jack Stewart, who had the original idea, for his encouragement and patience over the long months of giving birth to this book.

JNW
October 1969

Contents

CHAPTER 1

Footprints on the Moon

On the lonely, lifeless landscape of the moon, a strange-looking vehicle squats motionless under the sun's glaring rays. On one of its four spindly legs is attached a small, stainless steel plaque which reads:

HERE MEN FROM THE PLANET EARTH
FIRST SET FOOT UPON THE MOON.
JULY 1969 A.D.
WE CAME IN PEACE FOR ALL MANKIND.

The vehicle, the cast-off lower half of a lunar landing craft, is a monument to the historic event on July 20, when two American astronauts planted the first human footsteps on the moon.

The monument will stay there for ages, for there is no wind or water on the moon to wear it away.

The man who took the first step was Neil A. Armstrong, the 38-year-old civilian commander of the Apollo 11. As he reached the bottom of the landing craft's ladder and extended his booted left foot to touch the moon's powdery surface, he said: "That's one small step for a man, one giant leap for mankind."

He was followed down the ladder minutes later by Edwin E. Aldrin, Jr., a 39-year-old Air Force colonel. For 2 hours and 21 minutes, the two men, carefully at first and then boldly, wandered about on the barren, rock-strewn surface. They tested their ability to move about on this strange world. They took photographs of the landscape. They set up scientific experiments and collected rock and soil samples. They set up a television camera so the whole world could watch. At one point, Armstrong said to Aldrin, "Isn't this fun?"

All the while, the third member of the crew, Michael Collins, 38, an Air Force lieutenant colonel, piloted the Command Ship in lunar orbit 70 miles above the surface, waiting for the two explorers to rejoin him for the trip back to earth. Altogether, the visit to the moon lasted 21 hours and 37 minutes.

AN INCREDIBLE TRIUMPH

For the Apollo 11 crew, and for the United States space team, the successful 500,000-mile mission involving 88 separate steps was an incredible triumph of skill and courage. For the world, it was the most dramatic proof of what man can do if he puts his mind to it. The moon, which used to seem unreachable, was now within man's reach, the first port of call in the new age of spacefaring.

There have been other daring expeditions, of course. But

Apollo 11 was different: the world watched it as it happened. Through television and radio, hundreds of millions of people followed the activities aboard Columbia, the command ship, and Eagle, the landing craft—names chosen because, as Armstrong put it, they were "representative of the flight and the nation's hope." The television pictures across the 238,000 miles from the moon were so clear and sharp, showing the deep shadows and bright sunlight, that they seemed almost unreal.

Though the mission was completed almost without flaw, it was filled with suspense and anxiety. The astronauts faced risks on the moon never before met by man. And, as with all space flights, chances of failure and disaster were ever present—the blast-off of the giant Saturn 5 rocket at Cape Kennedy, the entry of the spaceship into earth and lunar orbits, the never-before-attempted landing and lift-off from the moon, the link-up of Columbia and Eagle, the re-entry into the atmosphere, the splash-down. An error or failure of any of the millions of individual parts anywhere along the way could have ended the mission short of the goal. An equipment failure or accident on the moon could have left the astronauts stranded.

HEROES

But they made it. After eight days in space, they splashed down in the Pacific to a presidential greeting aboard the recovery carrier, the U.S.S. Hornet. They were the heroes of the nation and the world.

"This is the greatest week in the history of the world since the Creation," President Nixon told the space travelers. "As a result of what you've done, the world has never been closer together before."

The welcome was not the familiar red-carpet ceremony of

space missions in which the returning astronauts walk across the deck of the carrier. The Apollo 11 crewmen were inside an isolation van and they talked with Mr. Nixon by microphone. The astronauts were under quarantine because of the slim chance that they brought back some deadly moon virus for which man has no immunity.

People everywhere were excited by this moon trip. Perhaps never before had one event so captured the world's imagination and spirit of adventure. There were some grumbles about problems to be solved here on earth, but for days Apollo was all over the headlines, TV sets, and radios throughout the world.

What moved the human spirit was, as Aldrin put it in a thoughtful moment on the way home, the "curiosity of all mankind to explore the unknown" that had sent explorers to brave the harshest conditions of this planet—to the poles, to the tops of mountains, to the loftiest balloon altitudes, to the deepest portions of the sea. Then why not the moon?

There were critics who said that the Apollo program cost too much, that the money and talent could be more usefully directed to fighting disease and poverty, that it was a "childish stunt" to make a race out of going to the moon. But by the time of the moon trip, many people began to think that the astronauts might bring back some clues to help solve the mysteries of the universe.

Whatever would be learned from the Apollo 11 voyage, it was a great expansion for mankind. It was a journey that took man beyond the earth to walk on another world.

CHAPTER 2

The Target

By the time the Apollo 11 astronauts began preparing for their lunar voyage, scientists had gathered enormous amounts of data about the moon. For thousands of years astronomers have been looking at the moon, studying its appearance and its motion through the sky. For the past 360 years, detailed views of the moon have been made possible through the use of telescopes. More recently, we have been able to reflect radar signals from the moon and to send scientific instruments to the moon on unmanned rockets. Radar signals and rockets able to travel through outer space are the products of our fast-moving scientific age, and they have shown us things about the moon that could never have been known before.

What, then, was known about the moon as the Apollo astronauts set out for their landing? What sort of world were they going to visit?

One way to picture the earth and the moon is to think of them as a pair of dancing partners spinning wildly around a dance floor with the sun in the center. Since the earth is 81 times as heavy as the moon, it is the anchor man in the dance.

Instead of keeping the same face toward its little dancing partner all the time, the earth spins like a top. This spin turns all parts of the earth toward the moon. The same spin also turns all parts of the earth toward the sun, giving us our day and night. A single spin of the earth takes about 24 hours—actually 23 hours and 56 minutes.

The moon spins much more slowly than the earth—so slowly that it always keeps the same face toward the earth. It makes one complete spin in the same amount of time that it takes to make a complete orbit around the earth. The time that the moon takes for a single orbit and a single spin is $27\frac{1}{3}$ days. This period of time has an old name—it is called a "month."

Astronomers have a down-to-earth way of illustrating the moon's motions. Stand in a room, they suggest, and place a chair in front of you. You are the moon; the chair is the earth. First, go all the way around the chair, always facing the same wall. That is *not* the way the moon moves, because you "orbited" but you did not spin. Now, go around the chair, facing the chair at all times. You will find that you orbited once around the chair, *and* you spun once. The same part of your body was always facing the chair. So it is with the moon and earth.

The way the moon always keeps its same side toward the earth comes about because the gravitational pull of the earth controls the motions of the moon. Each of the bodies is constantly affected by the other's presence. The tidal forces between the two, for instance, are unmatched elsewhere in the solar system. The moon's gravitational force causes earth's oceans to rise and fall and that is why we have high and low tides. Also, the earth's constant tugging has caused a definite bulge on the side of the moon that faces the earth. The earth is not a perfect ball either, but is a little bit pear shaped, and the moon's pull has partly caused that.

Other planets in the solar system have their moons, too. Jupiter, the largest of the nine planets, has twelve moons orbiting around it. The smallest of these is only 14 miles in diameter, and the largest is Ganymede, 3100 miles in diameter, the largest moon in the solar system. Saturn has ten moons, in addition to its amazing rings. The largest of Saturn's moons is Titan, 3,000 miles in diameter. Uranus has five moons, Neptune and Mars have two moons each, and Mercury and Venus have none. If far-away Pluto has any moons, they have not yet been observed. In fact, many astronomers think that Pluto may once have been a moon of Neptune until it escaped into its own orbit around the sun.

The earth-moon system is unusual, though, because the earth (with a diameter of 7,963 miles) is a comparatively small planet, while our moon (with a diameter of 2,160 miles) is a comparatively large moon. Therefore, astronomers often think of the earth-moon system as a double planet. This double planet, making a full orbit around the sun once every 365 days, may be one of the most beautiful systems in the universe. Of course, we cannot know that for certain, because we are not yet able to travel to another sun and see its family of planets. But we did take a step in that direction when the Apollo astronauts landed on the moon.

The moon has no detectable atmosphere—neither air nor any other gases. Therefore, it has no weather—no wind, no clouds, no rain, no snow, no water on the surface. People obviously have to take along their own air and water.

The moon's lack of atmosphere causes strange effects. Except for the voices and cracklings on their built-in radio sets and the sounds of their own breathing and motions, the astronauts hear nothing, because there is no air to carry sound waves. Also, there is no color in the moon's sky—only blackness, both day and night. (The blue of earth's sky is caused by particles of air scattering the sunlight.) By day a brilliant sun lights the surface of the moon. By day and night, stars shine in the black sky much more brightly than they do in our night sky. Stars seen from the moon do not twinkle—the twinkling that we are used to is caused by the starlight passing through the air.

Looking up from the moon's surface, the Apollo astronauts were able to see the great, shining earth. Since the earth is larger than the moon and a better reflector of sunlight, earthshine on the moon is more than eight times as bright as moonshine on the earth. If the astronauts had been on the moon for an entire month, they would have seen the earth go through different phases— crescent earth, half earth, and full earth. The phase of the earth (like the phase of the moon when we look at it) would depend on the direction that the sunlight was coming from and what portion of the sunlit part of the earth was visible at any time.

The earth's atmosphere protects people in many ways. Astronauts on the moon have to do without that protection. For instance, with no air to filter out some of the sun's heat, the surface of the moon is heated to a temperature of about 260 degrees Fahrenheit. Just how hot that is can be seen from the fact that water boils at the earth's surface at 212 degrees Fahrenheit. During the lunar night the temperature plunges to at least 240 degrees below zero Fahrenheit—low enough to freeze the mercury in a thermometer. That is because the moon does not have an atmosphere to act as a blanket, to hold much of the day's heat when the sun goes down. Visitors to the moon must also remember that, because of the moon's slower spin, lunar days and nights each last about two weeks of earth time.

In addition to light, there are dangerous radiations given off by the sun. These rays are made up of atomic-sized particles that do not reach earth because of the shielding air. But these rays do bombard the moon. A sudden flare-up of this radiation could be very dangerous to astronauts and they would have to take cover inside a shielded spacecraft or inside caves or other shelters on the moon.

Scientists are not sure whether the moon ever did have an atmosphere. If the moon did have an atmosphere billions of years ago, its weak gravity could not hold onto the gases and let them slip away into space. The moon's surface gravity is only about one-sixth as strong as earth's surface gravity.

The moon's low gravity has its advantages. For one thing, it would be easier to launch a rocket off the moon than off the earth. The moon's grip on objects is not as strong as earth's. This makes it possible for astronauts on the moon to lift heavier objects and take longer, springier steps than they could on earth. A person or object weighing 180 pounds on earth would weigh only 30 pounds on the moon. An astronaut would be able to leap 20 feet off the ground.

However, there is another kind of heaviness called "inertia" that has nothing to do with gravitational pull. The heavier an object is, the harder it is to stop it or make it turn once it is in motion, and the harder it is to start it moving when it is still. It is inertia that makes a big truck harder to stop, or turn, or get moving again, compared with stopping, turning, or pulling away from a stop in a small sports car.

Even though the *weight* of a person or an object on the moon would be much less, making enormous leaps and the lifting of very heavy objects possible, *inertia* would not change. An object on the moon would have just as much inertia as it would on earth. So, an astronaut making great leaps and bounds across the moon would find that it would be hard to turn or dodge or come to a stop. The result could be a dangerous crashing against things that might damage his spacesuit or break his bones. Therefore, astronauts on the moon do not make the great leaps that they could make.

THE LANDSCAPE OF THE MOON

When you look at the sunlit surface of the moon, you can see that there are both light and dark patches. It is the pattern of dark patches on the bright moon that people have seen as the outlines of an imaginary face—"the man in the moon."

Telescope studies of the moon show that the brighter areas are mountains and rugged highlands. The dark patches are smoother plains. The early astronomers thought that these plains were seas. They gave them such names as "Sea of Showers," "Sea of Clouds," and "Ocean of Storms." These names are still used, even though the so-called seas are now known to be dry, flat stretches of land.

Scientists have suggested various theories to explain how these great plains were formed on the moon. One theory is that they are great areas of dust caused by meteorites and dust particles striking the moon for billions of years—and some scientists thought that these dust layers were so deep and loose that they might swallow up anyone who landed there.

Another theory is that these plains were formed as spreading pools of molten lava. According to this theory, a large meteor hitting the moon would melt the surface rock by the force of the collision. The melted rock would flow, as lava, across the landscape, covering old craters and all but the highest peaks. Another possible source of the lava might have been the eruption of a volcano.

Still another theory is that these plains are dark areas because they are covered with the leftovers of plant life that might have existed on the moon billions of years ago. Dr. John J. Gilvarry of the National Aeronautics and Space Administration (NASA) originated this theory. He believed that the moon had true seas when it was young, but that they evaporated into mist, which drifted away into space because of the moon's weak gravity. But the seas might have been there long enough for life to develop. After the seas were gone, layers of this living material may have been left behind.

Scientists also have different theories about the lunar craters, the most striking features of the moon's surface.

Thousands of craters, ranging in diameter from the 160-mile-wide Clavius down to those no bigger across than a silver dollar, give the moon its scarred appearance. A person standing at the center of one of the broader craters would be unable to see the crater walls. That is because the moon, being smaller than earth, has a surface that curves more sharply.

Some of the craters are amazingly deep. The crater Newton is so deep (29,000 feet) that Mount Everest would barely peep out the top if it were set down there. No sunlight or earthshine ever casts a cheery ray on the dark floor of Newton. A number of craters, such as the 75-mile-wide Alphonsus, are a puzzle to astronomers because of the mountain peaks rising from their floors. These peaks are usually found near the centers of the craters and never seem to be as high as the surrounding walls. There are even craters within craters, as in the case of the central crater of the large crater Copernicus, the so-called "monarch of the moon." Typical of many "young" craters is Tycho Brahe, a 56-mile-wide depression in the south of the moon. Rays of very light materials stretch out from its rim, some for 1,000 miles. These rays seem to be the marks of the birth of the crater, and they are probably the splash marks left when dirt and rocks were flung outward. This sunburst effect makes Tycho one of the most brilliant sights on the moon.

Many scientists believe that lunar craters were formed by the collisions of meteors and comets against the moon. However, the case is not closed, and some scientists argue that the craters came from volcanic eruptions.

Other features of the landscape include the highlands and mountains, rills and ridges, deep faults and long valleys.

In the highlands, believed to be the oldest parts of the moon's surface, there are so many craters that they overlap. The broken fragments of crater walls seem to have piled up to form the surrounding rough landscape, and some of the ridges are thought to be leftover walls of old craters. From the edges of the plains, chains of mountains rise up. The largest, the Leibniz range, which lies near the south pole, has peaks up to 30,000 feet tall.

The rills of the moon, another common feature, are streaks or cracks that look like streams. They may have once been "river beds" for streams of red-hot lava. Deeper breaks or faults have also been seen. They may be a sign that the moon has violent "moonquakes" just as the earth has earthquakes.

Though it is popular to speak of the moon as a dead world, an orbiting cinder, scientists are not so sure. In 1956, a Russian astronomer, Nikolai A. Kozyrev, detected what seemed to be traces of gas flowing out of the crater Aristarchus. Two years later, his instruments showed a possible gas release from the crater Alphonsus. These observations show that there may be some active stirring just beneath the quiet-looking surface of the moon.

The scientific data brought back by the Apollo astronauts should help to solve many of these mysteries about the moon. By the time the data has been carefully studied, scientists may also know more about the birth of the moon. This question has been an important one in our century—where did the moon come from?

There are three theories about the birth of the moon. In the first, the moon is thought to have formed somewhere in space, after which it wandered until captured by the earth's gravitational field. The second theory is that the moon was once part of earth, then split off and went into orbit. In the third theory, the moon is believed to have developed as a separate body at the same time as earth, perhaps from materials left over from the formation of earth. But, whatever the birth of the moon was like, most scientists agree that the moon became a satellite of the earth soon after the two bodies were formed. That would make the moon about 4½ billion years old.

However the moon was formed, the fact that men would soon be able to visit it built up new scientific interest in earth's nearest neighbor. To many astronomers, the moon had seemed to be a dull, unchanging world compared with Mars or Jupiter or the distant stars. But the Apollo project changed that. People began to see the moon as a place for great discoveries. As the Nobel prizewinning scientist Harold C. Urey pointed out, the very slowly changing surface of the moon makes it a place where the marks of events billions of years old may still be seen. In that way, the moon is like a window into the very distant past. Robert Jastrow of NASA's Goddard Space Institute put it this way: "Because its surface has preserved the record of ancient events, it holds a key to the history of the solar system."

In the summer of 1965, a group of leading scientists from the National Academy of Sciences met at Woods Hole on Cape Cod, a place where men usually spend their time exploring the inner space of the oceans. The scientists were meeting to consider what the first men on the moon should do to gather as much valuable scientific information as they could in a short time. The scientists were interested in finding out many different things about the moon. They hoped that the astronauts would bring back information about the kinds of rock that the moon is made of, the causes of craters, the age of the moon, traces of volcanic activity, the number of meteors hitting the moon, measurements of radiation striking the moon from the sun and from outer space, and any traces of magnetism in the moon rocks.

Not all of the questions could be answered on the first landing, to be sure, but the instruments to be carried to the moon should be designed to find out as much as possible. The suggestions included an instrument to detect any tremors in the moon's surface, either from a moonquake, a volcanic eruption, or a meteor impact. The scientists also wanted the astronauts to bring back as many samples of lunar soil as possible. They also suggested an experiment to collect any gases spewed out by the sun to bombard the moon. They had other, more complicated suggestions, but NASA finally decided that setting up a quake detector, collecting rocks, and laying out a gas detector and other instruments would occupy enough of the time and energy of the first men on the moon.

With these scientific goals in mind, the United States began preparing a fleet of unmanned picture-taking spacecraft to scout out the moon in advance of the men of Apollo. These were the Ranger crash-landers, Surveyor soft-landers, and Lunar Orbiters (see Chapter 4). Besides sending back a wealth of intriguing scientific data, these robots would reassure Apollo planners that they knew how to get to the moon.

CHAPTER 3

Charting the Way to the Moon

In 1961, under the leadership of President Kennedy, the decision to build the Apollo moonship was made. It was clear, at that time, that the problem of how to build such a moonship was not going to be easily solved.

In the months following the Kennedy decision, five plans were being considered for the Apollo design. At first, the most popular method was "direct ascent." It seemed to be the simplest. A monster, three-stage rocket would blast a spaceship weighing about 150,000 pounds across space toward the moon. When it neared the moon, the spaceship would go into an orbit around the moon. Then, the ship's retro-rockets would fire.

The retro-rockets of an orbiting spaceship act as brakes. For a ship nose-first in orbit, the blasting retro-rockets, if aimed toward the line of flight, would send their flaming gases out in a forward direction, causing a backward push on the ship. This backward push would make the ship lose orbit energy and begin to spiral downward. For the moonship orbiting around the moon, the retro-blast would send it down toward the surface of the moon.

After the crew explored the moon, they would blast off in their spaceship and head back to earth.

This whole approach to visiting the moon had the advantage of being very simple and direct. But there was a disadvantage— an enormous amount of rocket power would be needed to do the job. The *direct-ascent* method would mean building a rocket nearly twice as powerful as the most powerful rockets in the world. It would be named the "Nova," and its rocket thrust at blast-off would be an enormous force measuring 13 million pounds.

But, it would be many years before the Nova could be built and tested. Besides, at that time, nobody was sure that the moon's crust would be strong enough to support the weight of the big 150,000-pound spaceship that the Nova would send to the moon. There was also a chance that such a tall ship (80 to 100 feet) might topple over when it made its moon landing. One NASA engineer said it would be almost like trying to land the Washington Monument on its base.

So, turning away from this simple, "brute force" approach, the designers began to think about a plan called "earth-orbit rendezvous." The American rocket specialist Wernher von Braun, who had come to this country from Germany to play an important part in space research, originally favored this method. Rather than launching the entire spaceship with a big Nova-type booster, smaller rockets would launch parts of the moonship. Perhaps five different sections of the moonship would be launched separately into orbit around the earth. Astronauts working in outer space would connect the orbiting sections to complete the building of the moonship.

While the *earth-orbit rendezvous* would do away with any need for the Nova rocket, it still left problems. The weight of the moonship, once it was put together in its earth orbit, would be about the same as it would be in the brute-force plan. So, the moon landing would be just as hard to do. Another problem was the split-second timing needed for the five separate launchings, in order for the sections of the moonship to come together for their orbital meeting or "rendezvous."

A different kind of rendezvous called the "tanker" method began to get a lot of scientific attention. The idea called for sending an unmanned tanker rocket into earth orbit. Then, the Apollo moonship would be sent into orbit by a Saturn 5 booster. The Apollo would use the tanker as an "orbital service station," docking at the tanker and getting filled with rocket fuel. Then it would separate from the tanker and rocket toward the moon. The advantage of this method would be that all the extra fuel supplied by the tanker would not have to be boosted from the launch pad with the moonship. It was one more way to use smaller boosters and stay away from the enormous Nova rocket. But fueling in orbit, especially using the super-cold liquid oxygen, seemed to be a complicated and risky operation.

A fourth possibility was "lunar-surface rendezvous." Extra fuel and supplies would be rocketed to the moon's surface on board unmanned spaceships. After the astronauts landed from a direct flight, they could refuel from the supplies that were waiting for them on the moon before they started their return flight to earth. But there would be serious risks. First, there would be no way of knowing if the supplies had landed without damage. There was the added risk that the astronauts might land too far from the supplies and would be unable to refuel. That would leave them stranded on the moon.

While scientists and government leaders were trying to decide among these four plans, a NASA engineer named John C. Houbolt suggested a fifth plan. His plan became known as "lunar-orbit rendezvous." According to this plan, a Saturn 5 rocket, launched from the earth, would boost the Apollo ship toward the moon, with a crew of three astronauts. Apollo would go into orbit around the moon. But the entire moonship would not land on the moon. Instead, a small landing craft would be separated from the moonship. The landing craft, carrying two astronauts, would use its retro-rocket to reach the moon's surface. The third astronaut would stay on board the main part of the moonship, orbiting around the moon while his crewmates explored the surface. When the exploration was completed, the two astronauts on the moon would blast off in the landing craft to join the moonship once more. Then, leaving the landing craft to orbit around the moon as an empty shell, the three astronauts would rocket back toward earth in the main part of the Apollo moonship.

The lunar lander would do for Apollo what a small boat does for a big ship. Rather than land a big ship on a shallow shore, it is more practical to anchor the ship offshore and use a boat to land on the beach. The same sort of idea fitted the *lunar-orbit rendezvous*. It would take a lot of rocket energy and fuel weight to land Apollo on the moon and then to blast off again from the moon's surface. By parking the Apollo in orbit and using the small landing craft, the landing could be carried out with a much smaller cost in rocket fuel. More weight would be saved by leaving the landing craft in orbit around the moon instead of having to carry its weight on the trip back.

Many Apollo planners thought that the lunar-orbit rendezvous was too risky. They were worried about the idea of the astronauts having to carry out the exact rendezvous maneuvers 230,000 miles from earth. Would it not be less risky, they asked, to try for rendezvous in earth orbit where, if anything went wrong, it would be easier to bring the men back to earth? Also, some scientists felt that the small landing craft would not be able to carry enough instruments for a thorough study of the moon's surface.

But, after much argument and study, it was decided that the lunar-orbit rendezvous had so many advantages that it was undoubtedly the best of the five methods. Its lower cost, the fact that it could be built in time for a moon trip in the late 1960's, and the fact that it was fairly simple to develop made it the best all-around choice.

Out of the smoke of battle came the first clear outline of how the United States would try to meet President Kennedy's pledge to reach the moon in the 1960's. Lunar-orbit rendezvous would be used. The booster at the launch pad would be a three-stage Saturn 5 rocket, with a thrust of $7\frac{1}{2}$ million pounds at lift-off. As each rocket stage used up all its fuel and burned out, it would be dropped off, so that the ship would not have to carry its useless weight. Then, the next stage would begin to burn.

Finally, with all three of the Saturn 5 stages burnt out and shed along the way, the Apollo moonship would be on its own, heading for the moon. The Apollo would be made up of three sections: the Command Module (where the three astronauts would ride), the Service Module (the equipment and rocket unit behind the Command Module), and the Lunar Module (the small spacecraft in which two men would ferry to and from the moon's surface).

Having made the decision of how to get to the moon, the Apollo Project planners were then faced with the enormous task of mobilizing the men and resources, designing and building the machines, and perfecting the techniques for the mission.

CHAPTER 4

Robot Pathfinders

Little was known about space travel in 1961. No American astronaut had even orbited the earth yet. No American spacecraft had journeyed to the moon. No one, neither the scientists nor the engineers, could be sure that the moon was a safe place for a landing.

Yet once the Apollo decision was made, we reached out in an incredibly short span of time to touch the moon. These first missions were carried out by robot spacecraft. They photographed the moon's surface, picked at its soil, and analyzed its rocks. They orbited around the moon many times, testing its gravitational forces and mapping good landing spots.

It was necessary to see what the moon was like, whether or

not it was safe to land men there and, if so, where would be the best landing sites. To answer these questions, the United States mounted three unmanned lunar exploration projects in the 1960's —Ranger, Surveyor, and Lunar Orbiter.

These robot scouting parties for Apollo were controlled from a quiet research center nestled against the San Gabriel Mountains on the outskirts of Pasadena, California. This is the Jet Propulsion Laboratory (JPL). One of the nation's oldest space research centers, it built the first American spacecraft, Explorer 1, and designed vehicles to pass by Venus and Mars as well as to go to the moon.

Exploring the moon with unmanned spacecraft turned out to be no easy task. The United States recorded twelve moonshot failures before finally succeeding with Ranger 7 in 1964. The Soviet Union was only slightly more successful. One of its vehicles, called Luna 2, smashed almost dead center into the front side of the moon on September 12, 1959, to become the first man-made object to touch another world. Three weeks later, Luna 3 flew around the back of the moon, returning the first photographs of the side always hidden from earth viewers. Though rather blurred and grainy, the pictures showed that the moon's far side, like its front, was pitted with craters. But after these successful missions, several Soviet moonflights met with failure in the years between 1959 and 1966.

RANGER

The Ranger Project, the first step in America's lunar exploration, was actually started before Apollo. In 1959, NASA officials asked JPL to design a spacecraft that could take close-up pictures of the moon's surface. The craft they had in mind would help scientists to learn about moonflight and would also give them a clear view of lunar features never before seen by man.

The JPL engineers came up with a ship that weighed about 800 pounds and, in flight, looked like a giant dragonfly. Ranger's wings were its two solar panels, extending 15 feet from tip to tip. These were designed to absorb the sun's energy and change it to electricity to run the spacecraft's instruments. The body of the spacecraft was ten feet long with an instrument section in the front and with a narrow tail where television cameras were mounted. With the new Atlas-Agena rocket as the launcher, the Ranger would first go into an earth orbit and then, with the refiring of the Agena, shoot out toward the moon, sending television pictures back to earth during the last 20 minutes of flight, before crashing into the lunar face.

The first two Rangers, launched in 1961, never got out of earth orbit. The Agena failed to restart. Three more Rangers, more advanced models than the first two, were launched in 1962. But they, too, were failures. An aiming error of the Atlas booster caused Ranger 3 to miss the moon by about 23,000 miles. Ranger 4's control system short-circuited, sending the spacecraft crashing into the far side of the moon. Ranger 5's power system went dead before it reached the moon. Ranger 6 followed a perfect course to the moon's Sea of Tranquility, but then it plunged toward the surface with its television cameras dead. There were no pictures.

Finally, Ranger 7 was launched on July 28, 1964. It worked. The 807-pound package of six television cameras beamed 4,300 pictures back to earth before hitting the Sea of Clouds. They showed craters as small as 3 feet in diameter and some rocks no more than 10 inches wide—features that no earth-based telescope could have picked out.

In 1965, Rangers 8 and 9 repeated Ranger 7's success, sending back 12,951 high-quality pictures of the moon. Ranger 8 photographed the Sea of Tranquility and Ranger 9 focused on the highlands area near the Sea of Clouds.

The Ranger pictures were the first evidence that many areas

of the moon were smooth enough for manned landings. Geologists were surprised, in fact, to find so few boulders and loose rocks on the lunar surface. Still, no one could be sure that the surface was firm enough to support a 15-ton landing craft. The pictures settled few of the scientific arguments over the nature of the moon's surface. People still did not know whether it was blanketed with dust, whether it was porous and crumbly, or whether its craters had been caused by volcanoes or by meteors.

SURVEYOR

It was left to a spidery, three-legged spacecraft called Surveyor to furnish a more spectacular and exact report on lunar conditions. The Surveyor was designed to land softly on the moon, photograph its immediate surroundings, test the "bearing strength," or firmness, of the lunar surface, and even run a chemical test of the soil.

Surveyor was the most complex piece of space machinery of its day. Into its triangular aluminum frame were packed fuel tanks, small guidance rockets, various sensing devices, and the guidance equipment on which the soft landing depended—radar, computer, autopilot, and the braking rocket. Its total weight at lift-off was at least 2,200 pounds. After finding its way across 240,000 miles of space, Surveyor was expected, on command from the ground, to point its braking rocket toward the moon at a slant. At about 200 miles above the surface, the on-board radar had to switch on and, at 60 miles, the radar had to order the braking rocket to fire. This blast was to slow Surveyor from a speed of 6,000 miles an hour to 250 miles an hour. Another radar, similar to one astronauts would later use for their lunar descent, would begin bouncing signals off the moon to help Surveyor feel its way to the surface. It was up to three smaller rocket engines to apply more braking thrust until the spacecraft was 14 feet off the lunar ground. Then, with all engines shut off, the craft would fall the rest of the way.

While Surveyor was still untried and unproven, the Soviet Union was also trying to land on the moon. Its first five soft-landing efforts were failures. Finally, on January 31, 1966, a Soviet spacecraft named Luna 9 reached the moon's surface in working order.

From Russian accounts, it appeared that Luna 9 was fairly crude compared to Surveyor. Just before it crashed on the moon, it tossed out a 220-pound sphere that was about twice the diameter of a basketball. As the sphere bounced onto the moon, its outer case dropped away like flower petals, exposing a single television camera. The spacecraft returned 27 pictures of rocks and soil before its batteries died.

About two months later, on April 3, Luna 10 became the first vehicle ever to go into orbit around the moon. The 3,500-pound spacecraft carried instruments to measure the moon's radiation and magnetism, if any, and to study the material of the moon's crust. But it apparently had no camera.

A study of Luna 10's data led to the first strong evidence that the moon, like earth, was once molten, and that its lighter rocks had risen to form a crust.

With high hopes, American space officials gathered at Cape Kennedy in May for the launching of the first Surveyor. On June 2, after a flight of more than 63 hours, Surveyor 1 landed softly on the Ocean of Storms near the crater Flamsteed. Its rotating television camera went into action and transmitted 11,150 black and white pictures before the long lunar night set in.

At a news conference in Washington after Surveyor's picture-taking days were over, Leonard Jaffe, JPL's project scientist, said: "The moon surface looks like a soil, not very hard, with rocks and clods on it and in it." Jaffe also said that the pictures showed clumps of material like wet soil. Such clumping was expected because small particles tend to stick together in a deep vacuum like that on the moon. Other scientists said they identified some pock-marked rock that looked like lava in which bubbles of gas have burst during cooling.

Four of the remaining six Surveyors were equally successful. They showed once and for all that the moon was a safe place for manned landings.

Surveyor 2 was launched in September, four months after the initial success and a month behind another Soviet moon-orbiting craft, Luna 11. This Surveyor was aimed at the Central Bay (Sinus Medii), but a failure of one of its maneuvering rockets sent it into a wild tumbling flight to crash landing.

Then, on April 3, 1967, Surveyor 3 landed gently on the Ocean of Storms and did more than take pictures. It stretched out a robot arm and dug a hole in the surface of the moon with a sharp metal claw. With slow, sometimes jerky movements, the mechanical arm extended itself nearly 5 feet on commands radioed from the control room on the earth. The experiment showed that lunar soil was fine-grained stuff that stuck together like damp clods.

Surveyor 4 was a failure. Signals stopped suddenly within 7 miles of the moon's Central Bay. Surveyor 5 landed successfully on the moon. Its measurements showed that the lunar rocks seemed to be like basalt, a material that forms the bedrock of the Palisades of the Hudson River, the Hawaiian Islands, and Iceland.

This was by far the most interesting of Surveyor's findings. It made scientists all the more eager to get their hands on the samples of lunar soil that the Apollo astronauts would bring back. It even made a few scientists pause and wonder if perhaps the scientist George Darwin had not been right when he suggested that the moon was a chunk of our planet that spun off from the Pacific basin when the earth was young.

Surveyor 6, which landed in the Central Bay on November 9 sent back more pictures and soil analysis. The last of the Surveyors, Surveyor 7, was aimed at the rugged highland region near Tycho, the relatively new and brightly rayed crater at the south of the moon's face. After Surveyor 7 landed on January 9, 1968, its instruments showed that there was less iron there than in the Sea of Tranquility, but otherwise the moonrock seemed to be about the same.

Thus, the Surveyors, after a slow start, proved to be excellent pathfinders for Apollo. Benjamin Milwitsky, the Surveyor program manager at NASA headquarters, said the awkward-looking vehicles "established that the moon is entirely suitable for Apollo landings. We've established that a spacecraft on the moon will not sink in deeply, that an astronaut will not need snowshoes to stay on top."

LUNAR ORBITER

At about the same time, another series of unmanned spacecraft—the Lunar Orbiters—were taking a different sort of look at the moon. From an orbit about 26 to 28 miles above the surface, they focused their cameras on a 3,000-mile strip along the lunar equator on the side visible to earth. This was the zone where astronauts would land, and Apollo planners wanted it completely mapped. All of the five Lunar Orbiters were successful in doing their mapping.

Compared to Surveyor, Lunar Orbiter was a fairly simple spacecraft. In flight, it looked a little like a four-leaf clover. The center section was the body, housing the camera, radio, and television equipment, and the rocket that fired the craft into lunar orbit. Sticking out from the body were two antennas and four solar panels—the four clover leaves. The 850-pound craft was launched by the Atlas-Agena rocket.

Lunar Orbiter 1 landed on August 10, 1966, and focused on nine promising Apollo landing sites to the south of the equator.

When Lunar Orbiter 2 began circling the moon on November 15, 1966, it made a similar survey of sites to the north of the equator. On February 8, 1967, the third Orbiter began re-examining the most promising Apollo sites, taking overlapping pictures that would bring out the shape of the surface.

Since the first three Orbiters were so successful, giving Apollo planners all they needed in the way of landing-site pictures, the last two flights were devoted to targets of great scientific interest. Both Orbiter 4 and Orbiter 5 circled the moon from its north pole to its south pole, rather than at its equator. In this way, they were able to photograph 99 per cent of the surface as it rotated under them. Orbiter 4 reached the moon in May of 1967; Orbiter 5 completed the series in August of that year.

One of the project's most important discoveries came from the way the Lunar Orbiters moved in their orbits. They had a curious way of dipping and wiggling when their orbits took them closest to the moon's surface. They were occasionally drawn three to six miles nearer the surface than they should have been. In 1968, after months of analysis, two JPL mathematicians—Paul M. Muller and William L. Sjogren—offered a reason when they noticed that the dips had happened during passes over circular crater-like seas—the Seas of Rains, Serenity, Crises, Nectar, and Moisture.

They reported that this dipping could be explained if there were large, dense concentrations of mass lying beneath these seas. They called the concentrations "mascons." According to one theory, the mascons could be the remains of meteors that had collided with the moon, melted from the heat of collision, cooled, and then settled into the moon's surface.

By the end of 1967, NASA had narrowed to five the number of promising sites for the first astronaut landing. Two were in the Sea of Tranquility, one on the eastern side, one in the Central Bay, and two more on the western side of the Ocean of Storms. As the robot pathfinders had discovered, these were safe, firm, and fairly smooth areas.

CHAPTER 5

Human Pathfinders

Beyond our sheltering atmosphere lie the great stretches of space. Space is airless and seems to be completely empty. But it is not exactly true that it is empty because it is flooded with invisible radiation.

Men in space must take their own air with them in order to breathe. They must be protected from extreme heat when the sun is shining on their ship and from extreme cold when the ship lies in the shadow of the earth or moon. They must learn to live in "free fall," the weightless condition in an orbiting ship where there is no feeling of up or down. Only when the ship's rocket blasts does there seem to be any up or down—then the force of the blast makes the back end of the ship seem like a floor. The rest of the time, the astronauts drift in their cabin like goldfish in a bowl.

Before the first men went into space, some scientists wondered if people could stand such strange conditions. Some thought that the astronauts might be very confused by the silence and loneliness and the floating, weightless condition in an orbiting spaceship. Others thought the human bones and heart might be damaged if astronauts were in free fall for a long time. The heart might be weakened by having too little work to do and might not be able to stand the strain of coming back to earth. There were also those who feared that the bones would begin to lose calcium, as happens when a person lies in bed for weeks. And—who could tell?—there might be other types of damage that no one would expect.

However, a larger number of scientists felt that conditions in a spaceship would not seriously harm astronauts—at least in short flights.

But what about the difficulty of getting men into space? Could engineers check on all the things that could go wrong and build spacecraft safe enough for human passengers? No one could be sure in 1961. Every so often a rocket would blow up in flames on the launching pad. Spacecraft got into orbit and then, when some electrical part failed, went dead. There was the question of building a ship light enough to get into space but strong enough to stand radiation, collisions with meteorites the size of sand grains, and the heat and vibrations of the return to earth.

The only way to be sure that Americans could build and fly space vehicles designed to carry human beings was to do it. This was the main purpose of the two manned flight projects that went before Apollo—Mercury and Gemini.

MERCURY

"We are behind," President Kennedy said after the Soviet

Union's Yuri Gagarin orbited the earth in April, 1961, in Vostok 1, "and it will be some time before we catch up."

It took about ten months.

On May 5, 1961, Alan B. Shepard, Jr., became the first American to venture into space—but it was far short of an orbital flight. He rode a Mercury spacecraft 302 miles down range from the Florida launching pad. During his fifteen minutes in space, he reached a height of 115 miles above the ground. Both the astronaut and the capsule were recovered in the ocean, proving that both could stand a short space flight. Shepard was in a weightless state only about four minutes. "The only complaint I have," said Shepard, "was the flight was not long enough."

Less than three months later, on July 21, 1961, Virgil I. "Gus" Grissom piloted another Mercury capsule along the same suborbital path. When Grissom splashed down, the explosive mechanism on the escape hatch went off accidentally, blowing the hatch open. Grissom swam free and was rescued by a waiting helicopter, but the capsule sank.

Both Shepard and Grissom had been launched by Redstone rockets, which were not powerful enough to boost them into orbit. The more powerful Atlas booster was still undergoing test firings with Mercury capsules, holding chimpanzees and robots. Until the Atlas was tested and ready, no Americans could become true orbiting spacemen.

The Soviet Union put its second manned spaceship into orbit two weeks after Grissom's flight. Gherman S. Titov, a 26-year-old Air Force major, circled the earth 17 times at altitudes from 110 to 160 miles and returned safely, touching down on land inside the Soviet Union. Titov's flight raised some doubts about man's ability to stand spaceflight. Titov wrote later: "For the life of me, I could not determine where I was. I felt suddenly as though I were turning a somersault and then flying with my legs up. I was completely confused, unable to define where was earth or the stars . . . My sense of orientation vanished abruptly and completely."

John H. Glenn, Jr., was the first American astronaut to make an orbital flight. After weeks of delay, he finally walked out to the launching pad before dawn on February 20, 1962. Thousands watched the Atlas and Mercury from the Canaveral beaches. Millions more throughout the country sat before television sets. At 9:17 A.M. the Atlas gave a thunderous roar and slowly rose.

Unlike Titov, Glenn found that the feeling of weightlessness was very pleasant. He never felt at all uncomfortable. He had no difficulty taking food from squeeze tubes. And he said that the view was "tremendous."

The flight had some tense moments. During the first three orbits, trouble developed with the small rockets that automatically controlled the tilt of the capsule. Glenn took over manual control of the rockets. Also, in the control room, a warning light showed that the capsule's plastic-glass heat shield had become unlatched. If the shield fell off, Glenn would be incinerated when the capsule plunged back into the earth's atmosphere.

A decision was made not to drop off the retro-rockets after they were fired. The hope was that the straps attached to the retro-pack, the unit holding the retro-rockets, which passed over the heat shield, might hold the shield in place. When the Mercury—Glenn called it Friendship 7—re-entered the atmosphere, the retro-pack flew off in "big, flaming chunks." Watching them sail past the capsule window, Glenn felt that the heat shield might be coming apart. Still, he stayed calm. "Boy, that was a real fireball," he reported to Mercury control. But the shield stayed in place, and Glenn's capsule hit the water near the recovery ship. After three orbits of earth, Glenn reported, "My condition is excellent."

What was this Mercury capsule like that these astronauts had flown so successfully? The main body of Mercury was shaped like a bell. It was 9 feet 7 inches long from the base of the blunt heat shield to the tip of the barrel-shaped nose. It was 6 feet 2 inches wide at its widest point, the blunt end, and weighed about 3,000 pounds. The nose contained radio antennas and control systems as well as the parachutes for landing. Mounted on the blunt end were the three retro-rockets needed to brake the spacecraft for the descent to earth. To save weight, the engineers decided that the cabin atmosphere should be pure oxygen at about one-third the pressure at sea level instead of a mixture of nitrogen and oxygen, which is more like normal atmosphere.

After Glenn's flight, three more astronauts took their turns orbiting in the Mercury. On May 24, 1962, M. Scott Carpenter became the second American to circle the earth. His three-orbit trip ended in suspense. As a result of a re-entry error, Carpenter's capsule overshot its landing point by 250 miles and, for a time, was out of radio contact with the recovery ship. But soon, the astronaut was found safe in his capsule. The mission was a success.

On October 3, 1962, Walter M. Schirra, Jr., took the next ride in Mercury. It lasted nine hours as he circled the earth six times in the most flawless mission to date.

The project was brought to a successful conclusion in May, 1963, with the 22-orbit, 34-hour flight of L. Gordon Cooper, who, at 36, was the youngest of the original seven astronauts. Toward the end of Cooper's flight, a failure in the equipment forced the astronaut to take over the controls himself. He manually guided the craft all the way down to a bulls-eye splashdown. "Right on the old gazoo," Cooper radioed.

Cooper's was the last of the Mercury flights. After six manned voyages, lasting a total of 51 hours and 40 minutes, Mercury had served its purpose. Men had gone into space and survived. Besides, they seemed able to work and think while in orbit and there had been no bad effects.

The Mercury Project had scarcely ended before the Soviet Union launched yet another Vostok, its fifth. After the Gagarin and

Titov missions in 1961, the Russians had outdistanced Mercury with a four-day manned flight in August, 1962. Andrian Nikolayev rode Vostok 3 for 64 orbits. While Nikolayev was aloft, Pavel Popovich was launched in Vostok 4 for a three-day, 48-orbit flight. The launching was timed and aimed so that Vostok 4 came within 3.1 miles of Vostok 3. For the fifth Vostok mission, nearly a year later in June, 1963, Valery Bykovsky orbited the earth 81 times and was joined in space by the first woman cosmonaut, Valentina Tereshkova, in Vostok 6. Though they did not accomplish a rendezvous, the two cosmonauts landed safely two and a half hours and 50 miles apart.

GEMINI

Gemini was a two-man spacecraft in which astronauts showed that they could steer through many of the maneuvers necessary for a flight to the moon. The Gemini spacecraft was larger and more maneuverable than the Mercury. The crew capsule was shaped a little like a bell and it had a blunt end shielded against fiery re-entry. It was 11 feet high and 7½ feet wide at the base. The weight of the capsule and its equipment unit was more than 7,000 pounds. The capsule contained radar for rendezvous maneuvers and a computer the size of a hatbox to solve in-flight problems.

The first two Gemini flights were unmanned tests of both the rocket, the more powerful Titan 2 military missile, and the spacecraft. No attempt was made to return and recover Gemini 1, launched into orbit on April 8, 1964. The second unmanned flight, in January, 1965, demonstrated successfully the craft's ability to withstand the heat and stress of re-entry.

Meanwhile, the Russians orbited the world's first multi-man spaceflight—three men in Voskhod 1, which circled the earth 16 times in October, 1964. And, on March 18, 1965, before Gemini 3 could be launched, the Russians sent up Voskhod 2 for a 17-orbit flight. It had two men aboard and one of them, Alexei Leonov, became the first human being to step outside an orbiting vehicle for a floating "walk" in space.

Less than a week later, on March 23, Grissom and John W. Young, a member of the second "class" of astronauts, selected in 1962, were launched in Gemini 3. Though it was a short flight —3 orbits—the two men had time to show that Gemini could be steered up and down, right and left, backward and forward, and could even change orbits. A set of sixteen thruster rockets ringing the vehicle made this possible.

On June 3, Gemini 4 was launched on a 4-day, 62-orbit flight during which Edward H. White became the first American to "walk" in space. White enjoyed his space walk so much that it took a little coaxing by his commander, James A. McDivitt, to get him back inside the capsule. For 20 minutes, he chatted, joked, and snapped pictures as he darted about in raw space, using a gas-firing jet gun to move from place to place. The bursts from the gun caused a recoil that pushed him in the opposite direction. Of course, that is the same thing that makes a rocket work. The recoil from the rocket blast is what pushes the ship forward. The same kind of force is at work when you let go of a rubber balloon full of air, with an untied neck. It is the recoil from the air squirting out through the neck of the balloon that makes it dart crazily through the air.

Next came Gemini 5. Cooper, the Mercury astronaut, and Charles P. Conrad, Jr., a rookie, began their planned 8-day mission on August 21, 1965.

A chemical "fuel cell" was used in Gemini 5 instead of an electric battery. The fuel cell, which used chemical reactions to generate electricity, was lighter than the batteries used in earlier flights. A fuel-cell system was already being planned for Apollo.

Early in the first day of Gemini 5's flight, the fuel cell began to fail. The astronauts flew a perfect mission anyway. The flight surgeon reported later that they had come through their 8-day trip in perfect health.

In December, 1965, Gemini 6 and Gemini 7 were launched and met each other in orbit. On board Gemini 6 were astronauts Schirra and Thomas P. Stafford. Gemini 7 was manned by Frank Borman and James A. Lovell, Jr. The two crafts came within a foot of each other and, for several hours, circled the earth in formation. "A piece of cake," Schirra said afterward, describing the beautiful rendezvous maneuvers.

Even a close shave on March 16, 1966, did not stop the Gemini team. On that date Gemini 8 was launched and made the first docking with another orbiting vehicle, a 27-foot-long unmanned Agena. It was "like parking a car," Neil A. Armstrong, the command pilot, said.

Then trouble struck. Gemini 8 began bucking and spinning wildly because of a misfiring thruster rocket. Armstrong and David R. Scott, the other crew member, were forced to make an emergency splashdown in the Pacific before the end of their first day in space.

In the last four Gemini flights, astronauts practiced over and over the techniques of rendezvous and docking and gained more experience operating outside their orbiting craft.

Gemini 9 was the three-day mission in which Stafford and Eugene A. Cernan used three different approaches to rendezvous with a target. No docking was tried because the protective clamshell shroud failed to break free of the target's docking collar. With jaws wide open, it looked to Stafford like "an angry alligator." Cernan performed a long space walk before the flight ended on June 6.

Young and Michael Collins took a 3-day trip in Gemini 10, beginning July 18. They achieved the first double rendezvous, first with their Agena and then with the still-orbiting Agena left over from the Gemini 8 mission. They docked with their own Agena.

On September 12, Gemini 11 was launched. During its 3-day flight, Conrad and Richard F. Gordon, Jr., linked up with an Agena and then fired the Agena's main engine to propel themselves 850 miles out from earth, the farthest man had ventured at the time.

For the last Gemini flight (Gemini 12), Lovell and Edwin E. Aldrin, Jr., raced into orbit on November 11 and, despite a balky radar unit, steered their craft to a successful rendezvous and docking with an Agena. They splashed down 4 days later, after many rendezvous maneuvers and Aldrin's $5\frac{1}{2}$ hours of space walking.

In the ten manned Gemini flights, American astronauts spent a total of 969 hours and 56 minutes in space. The experience in rendezvous and docking was important to Apollo planning, because the landing craft and the Apollo would have to rendezvous and dock in lunar orbit before the return to earth. The long Gemini flights also proved that man could survive in space for the 7 or 8 days it should take for a round trip to the moon. The Gemini space walks gave astronauts a feeling of what it would be like to work in the low-gravity conditions that exist on the moon and were good practice for emergency operations if there were any trouble docking in lunar orbit.

CHAPTER 6

The Men
Who Were Lost

From November, 1963, through the end of 1965, there were ten unmanned launchings in which various Apollo systems were tested. In the first full-scale unmanned test, on February 26, 1966, the spacecraft, including the Command Module and the Service Module, was fired 5,500 miles down the Atlantic Missile Range by a Saturn 1-B, forerunner of the Saturn 5. The rocket engine needed for lunar-orbiting maneuvers was fired and refired but did not blast at full power. Even so, Apollo officials rated the flight a "successful first step."

Two more tests were run in the summer of 1966. On July 5, a dummy payload was put into earth orbit to test the rocket stage that would boost men out of near-earth orbit toward the moon.

This was the engine S-4B that would be the third stage of the Saturn 5. The test was successful. Equally successful was a second launching on August 25, when an unmanned Apollo rose from Cape Kennedy on an 18,000-mile flight that ended in a Pacific Ocean splashdown. The spacecraft's engine fired perfectly and the heat shield withstood the temperature and pressure of a re-entry from space into the air.

The spacecraft for the first manned Apollo mission was shipped to Cape Kennedy in the summer of 1966. Then, came many months of testing and repairing troubles in the spacecraft. These difficulties went on for about a half a year. On January 27, 1967, three astronauts entered the Apollo capsule for ground tests. In these tests, the Apollo would never leave the ground and the rocket engines of the Saturn 1-B would not even be fired. The astronauts who were carrying out these tests were Roger B. Chaffee, a 31-year-old lieutenant commander in the Navy, Edward H. White, a 36-year-old lieutenant colonel in the Air Force, and Gus Grissom, also an Air Force lieutenant colonel and a veteran of two spaceflights—the second Mercury and the first Gemini.

On that Friday afternoon, the three fully suited astronauts lay strapped in the couches of Apollo 1—Grissom on the left, White in the middle, and Chaffee on the right. The spacecraft was perched on top of the Saturn 1-B, the two of them standing a total of 224 feet tall. Around it was the protective steel latticework of the 310-foot-high service tower, which provided platforms for workmen. Test conductors kept instrument watch on Apollo 1 from the "white room," the enclosed uppermost platform nearest the spacecraft, and from a blockhouse about 1,000 feet away.

Apart from the rocket's not being loaded with fuel, it was a realistic rehearsal of how the final countdown was to go. It was not considered a "hazardous" test because of the unloaded rocket. So everyone was somewhat relaxed and there were no emergency crews of firemen and doctors on hand.

With the astronauts inside the spacecraft, the hatch had been closed and sealed and the cabin pumped full of pure oxygen to a pressure of 16.7 pounds a square inch, 2 pounds higher than normal sea-level atmosphere. This was the way Apollo was to be pressurized while awaiting lift-off. Then there had come many delays as different things went wrong with various pieces of electrical equipment.

By 6:30 P.M., the countdown was finally moving along. Then, there came a sudden and terrible interruption. An electrical spark or short circuit inside the oxygen-rich cabin flooded the cabin with fire. The entire inside of the cabin filled with flames and smoke. There was no way to open the hatch quickly, either from the inside or from the outside. The three astronauts had soon died.

Slowly, after the shock of the launch-pad tragedy, the Apollo planners and engineers began to redesign the system. New safeguards (such as a quick-opening hatch) were built into the Apollo.

Plans were laid for a new flight, with Schirra, Walter Cunningham, and Donn Eisele as the crew. As the people of Apollo picked up the pieces, the memory of Grissom, White, and Chaffee was real and haunting. But what the Apollo people remembered more and more was not the astronauts' deaths but something Grissom had said. "If we die," he once had said, "we want people to accept it. We are in a risky business, and we hope that if anything happens to us it will not delay the program. The conquest of space is worth the risk of life."

THE RUSSIANS ALSO MEET WITH TRAGEDY

Until 1967, Russian cosmonauts had gone into space in two classes of spacecraft, the Vostoks and Voskhods. There were six manned missions in a Vostok (two each in 1961, 1962, and 1963) and two flights in a Voskhod (one each in 1964 and 1965). But such was the secrecy of the Soviet program that not until a few years later did Westerners get a fairly clear picture of these vehicles and their launching rockets.

The one-man Vostok was large and spherical and weighed roughly 10,400 pounds, about 3½ times as much as the Mercury. Vostok was roomier than Mercury. Its diameter was about 8 feet. There were two compartments, one for the pilot and one for the equipment. Those who had been inside a Vostok cockpit described it as much simpler than Mercury's, apparently containing fewer dials, gauges, and switches. One major difference was the cabin atmosphere. Instead of the low-pressure pure oxygen that American astronauts breathed, the Vostok cabin was pumped full of mixed gases (24 per cent oxygen and the rest primarily nitrogen) to a pressure almost like that at sea level. In other words, it was almost identical to the air we ordinarily breathe. The thicker walls of Vostok made it possible to maintain such a pressure, which might have ruptured the thin Mercury walls. Like the American craft, Vostok was equipped with braking rockets and parachutes for the return to earth. But it was designed so that when it got near the ground, the hatch opened automatically and, moments later, the pilot in his seat was explosively ejected. He came down to earth by parachute as the capsule floated down a separate chute.

The Russians shifted from the Vostok series to the Voskhod flights after they developed more powerful rockets. Western space experts think that the Voskhod was nothing but an improved Vostok. The same 8-foot sphere was rearranged so that three astronauts could sit side by side. The first manned Voskhod, sent aloft in October, 1964, weighed 11,731 pounds and carried a crew of three.

The second Voskhod, launched 5 months later, was heavier, weighing 12,529 pounds. It was heavier, although it carried two cosmonauts instead of three, because it included a submarine-like airlock. It was through this chamber that Alexei A. Leonov crawled to begin man's first "walk" in raw space. (This happened before the Gemini space walks.) When it came time for re-entry from orbit, Voskhod 2's automatic system failed to work properly. The cosmonauts had to wait another orbit and then steer the ship down to earth. Instead of landing in the open country of the Ukraine, where recovery teams were waiting, they came down far to the north in a snowbound forest. It took hours for the ship to be found and about a day for ground parties to break through the isolated woods to reach the crew and bring them out on skis.

Then came the launch of an advanced Soviet spacecraft, the Soyuz, on April 23, 1967, and in that mission, death came to a Soviet cosmonaut. His name was Vladimir M. Komarov and he had already been on a space mission in Voskhod 1.

The Soyuz had a disastrous re-entry from space. According to Soviet reports, Komarov died when the Soyuz plunged through the atmosphere and, with the parachute lines hopelessly tangled, crashed into the ground.

Many Russians broke into tears when the news was broadcast. The tragedy was a great shock to the Russian people, who had looked to the flight to help them regain their space leadership. There had been talk of a whole series of Soyuz missions throughout the summer. But now that this accident had happened, the Soyuz spacecraft would have to be studied and improved.

The three American astronauts and the one Russian cosmonaut who died inside their spaceships were brave men. Their calm and strength in carrying out dangerous missions were among the good qualities that they were chosen for. They died because it was important to them that man be able to explore the great universe around him—important enough so that they were ready to risk their lives for it.

CHAPTER 7

The
Saturn-Apollo

The Apollo spaceship, mounted on top of the Saturn 5 booster, is called the "Saturn-Apollo." There are many parts to the Saturn-Apollo, and, to understand the things that happened in the first moon trip, it is useful to know about these parts and how they work.

Everything about the Saturn 5 is big. When topped with the Apollo spacecraft, the three-stage rocket stands 363 feet tall, six stories higher than the Statue of Liberty. Its first, or booster stage, is the biggest aluminum cylinder ever machined. Its valves are as big as barrels, its fuel pumps are bigger than refrigerators, its fuel lines are big enough for a man to crawl through, and its engines are the size of trucks.

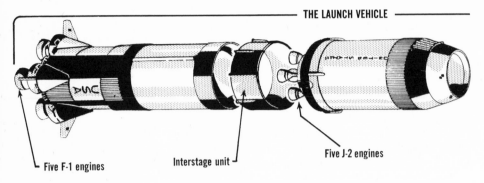

THE LAUNCH VEHICLE

Five F-1 engines   Interstage unit   Five J-2 engines

Five F-1 engines: Launch vehicle with 7.5 million pounds of thrust. **Interstage unit:** Connects first two stages and contains equipment for both. **Five J-2 engines:** Take rocket to altitude for earth orbit with more than a million pounds of thrust. **Single J-2 engine:** Puts vehicle into orbit with 200,000 pounds of thrust.

There are four main sections to the Saturn 5. The first-stage rocket is the biggest of these sections. As the tail-end section of the Saturn-Apollo, it is the first rocket to blast. Therefore, its blast must be powerful enough to lift the entire Saturn-Apollo up from the launch pad and hurl it toward outer space. It does not do this great task by using any special fuel mixture. In fact, it uses a mixture that is a fairly old-fashioned rocket fuel: liquid oxygen and kerosene.

By itself, the stage is bigger than any single previous rocket —138 feet tall and 33 feet in diameter. Its weight is more than three-quarters the weight of the entire Saturn-Apollo.

Clustered at the base of the stage are five engines, each 18 feet tall, that burn all their fuel in $2\frac{1}{2}$ minutes to force a fiery exhaust out their five bell-shaped nozzles. In these $2\frac{1}{2}$ minutes, the five engines use as much fuel as three million automobiles would use if they ran for $2\frac{1}{2}$ minutes each. Each engine blasts with 1.5 million pounds of thrust, making the total rocket thrust of the stage 7.5 million pounds.* With this power, it boosts the

---

* The thrusting force of a rocket is measured in pounds. A one-pound force is the force that would barely lift a one-pound weight off the ground. A one-million-pound thrust would barely lift a one-million-pound weight off the ground. A rocket engine must have enough thrust to lift a spaceship off the ground *and* to speed it upward.

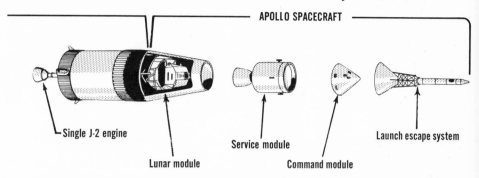

APOLLO SPACECRAFT

Single J-2 engine

Lunar module

Service module

Command module

Launch escape system

Lunar module: On lunar flight, will take two astronauts to the surface of the moon. **Service module:** Contains support systems for command module and power to maneuver it. **Command module:** "Home" for the three astronauts on their way to the moon and back. **Launch escape system:** Carries command module free of rocket in case of accident.

Saturn-Apollo 38 miles through the air to a speed of almost 6,100 miles an hour. Then, the burnt-out first stage disconnects and drops away.

Perched on the shoulders of the booster is the second stage, the most powerful hydrogen-fueled rocket ever built. It is 81 feet 7 inches high and 33 feet in diameter, and has five rocket engines. Its tanks hold 267,700 gallons of super-cold liquid hydrogen and 87,000 gallons of liquid oxygen, or "Lox." Unlike air-breathing jet engines, rocket engines carry their own oxygen** supplies. Otherwise, out in airless space, they could not fire at all.

The five engines of the second stage were designed to develop up to 225,000 pounds of thrust each, or 1,125,000 pounds for the entire stage. They burn for about 6 minutes, pushing the Saturn-Apollo to an altitude of about 115 miles and a speed of 15,300 miles an hour—just short of orbit. Then, they too burn out and drop away.

The third and uppermost stage of the Saturn 5 blasts the fast-moving ship into orbit. The third stage is 58 feet 7 inches high and 21 feet 8 inches in diameter, and carries 63,000 gallons of liquid hydrogen and 20,000 gallons of liquid oxygen.

** Some rockets use other chemicals in place of oxygen.

The stage's single engine fires when the vehicle is approaching orbit. By firing more than 2 minutes, boosting the ship's speed to 17,400 miles an hour, the third-stage rocket blasts the ship into orbit. On a voyage to the moon, the engine burns again for about 5 minutes to boost the astronauts out of their low earth orbit and on the way to the moon.

Finally, there is a 3-foot-high section on top of the Saturn 5 that is the rocket's electronic brain. Signals from this computer send instructions to the different stages, to ignite and shut down the engines and to check on their operation.

Just to get the many parts of the Saturn 5 to Cape Kennedy was a hard task. The first stage went by special barge from the Mississippi Test Facility on the Gulf of Mexico. The second stage was shipped by barge from California through the Panama Canal. The third stage and other smaller parts were sent to the Cape in an oversized transport plane called the "Super Guppy." They were all put together—"mated," as the engineers called it—in a 525-foot-tall building near the launching pad.

Inside this building, the Saturn 5's took shape, stage by stage. Once a Saturn 5 rocket was put together, it had to be moved out to the launch pad. A special, strong roadway had to be built, packed with river rocks. Along this road, a huge tractor-like vehicle as big as a baseball diamond carried the Saturns to their launch pads. The 3½-mile journey to the launch pad was nearly 8 hours long.

On November 9, 1967, the Saturn 5 was used to boost an unmanned model of Apollo into space. This test was the Apollo 4 mission. When the launch countdown reached zero, the five engines of the first stage fired, sending gushes of orange flame and smoke over the launching pad. A million gallons of water rushed into the concrete "flame bucket" underneath to prevent serious damage to the pad. As soon as instruments showed that all five engines were firing evenly, the steel "hold arms" on the nearby mobile tower loosened their grip on the spaceship. At 7 A.M., on schedule, the

36-story spaceship began to rise from its pad in a mushroom of smoke.

Not until the rocket cleared the launch tower, about 10 seconds after lift-off, did the shock wave reach the press site 16,000 feet away. It traveled through the ground and the air. The roar of Saturn 5 shook the small wooden grandstand, rattled its iron roof, and pushed in the plate glass window on a CBS mobile studio. Reporters in the open could feel the pressure of the shock wave beating at their faces and chests. Inside the launch control center, everything was covered with plaster dust that had shaken loose from the ceiling.

Each of the Saturn's three stages fired on schedule. When the third stage stopped burning, 11 minutes after lift-off, the unmanned Apollo spacecraft that had been on top of the rocket was orbiting earth. Unlike the other stages, the third one remained attached to the spacecraft. Later, it refired to drive the spacecraft 11,286 miles out from earth.

The rocket's third stage and a dummy lunar module, taken along to make it a realistic test of the full Saturn-Apollo, were then dropped away. On a signal from ground controllers, the Apollo's main rocket fired to ram the command module back down through the air at a speed of about 24,500 miles an hour, the speed it would travel on a return from the moon. This gave the command module's heat shield its first test at such re-entry speeds and temperatures. After a mission of 8 hours and 40 minutes, the command module splashed down in the Pacific northwest of Hawaii.

The second flight of the Saturn 5 was less successful. On April 4, 1968, another Saturn 5 was launched in a test of the rocket and of the Apollo spacecraft—the Apollo 6 mission. But two of the second stage engines burned out too soon and the third stage engine failed to reignite in orbit.

For a time, it appeared that NASA would have to conduct a third unmanned Saturn 5 launching before the mighty rocket could be "man-rated"—cleared for launching men. But engineers found out that the engine troubles were caused by vibrations that could easily be prevented.

The Saturn 5, the most powerful rocket in the world, was ready to launch astronauts into space.

THE LANDING BUG

The lunar module of the Apollo is a strange, awkward-looking craft. It has an oddly shaped body mounted on four spindly, jointed legs. It looks like a live creature, and that is why people have called it the "spider," the "moonbug," or the "landing bug." Compared with the huge, streamlined Saturn 5, and the smooth, cone-shaped Apollo command module, the lunar module is the ugly duckling of the Apollo mission.

There were reasons for the lunar module's strange shape. It was built entirely for flight in outer space—from the orbiting Apollo down to the moon, and then back up again, from the moon to rejoin Apollo. It never had to fly through the air, so it did not need a sleek, streamlined shape. During the launch phase, it would ride in a protective aluminum shell. After its mission on and around the airless, low-gravity moon, it was to be left in space.

So, the landing bug was built in a form that best fitted its mission. Since its mission was to land on the moon and spring off again, it was most practical to build it as a squat object with legs. Its squat shape would make it very steady as it landed, and its springy legs would cushion the landing. Then, when it was time for the two astronauts to leave the moon and join the Apollo, the landing bug would blast off into space once more. But, its lower half, including its legs, would no longer be needed. So, they would be left standing on the moon like the shed husk of a gigantic insect.

From the crew compartment of the bug, the astronauts could

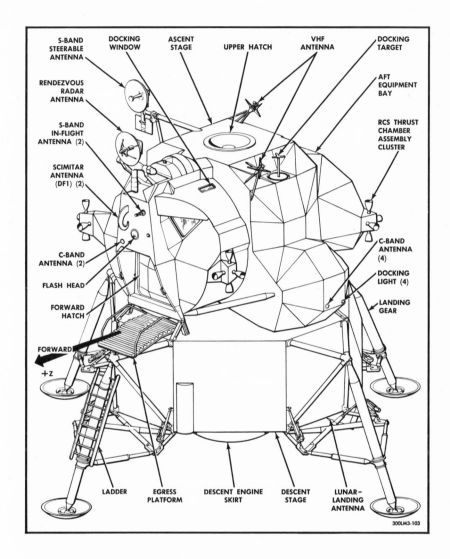

S-BAND
STEERABLE
ANTENNA

DOCKING
WINDOW

ASCENT
STAGE

UPPER HATCH

VHF
ANTENNA

DOCKING
TARGET

RENDEZVOUS
RADAR
ANTENNA

AFT
EQUIPMENT
BAY

S-BAND
IN-FLIGHT
ANTENNA (2)

RCS THRUST
CHAMBER
ASSEMBLY
CLUSTER

SCIMITAR
ANTENNA
(DF1) (2)

C-BAND
ANTENNA (2)

C-BAND
ANTENNA
(4)

DOCKING
LIGHT (4)

FLASH HEAD

FORWARD
HATCH

LANDING
GEAR

FORWARD

+z

LADDER

EGRESS
PLATFORM

DESCENT ENGINE
SKIRT

DESCENT
STAGE

LUNAR–
LANDING
ANTENNA

300LM3-103

look out through a pair of triangular windows. To save weight, there were no seats for the men; they would stand, loosely harnessed by straps. In front and on either side of them were the control panels for the LM's guidance, communications, environment, and propulsion systems. Above the commander's position, on the left side, was a window through which he could look to steer the bug back for the rendezvous and docking with the command module. At the astronauts' feet was the 42-inch-square forward hatch through which they would leave the bug to walk on the moon's surface.

COMMAND MODULE

Sometimes called merely the Apollo, the command module was a much roomier capsule than either the one-man Mercury or the two-man Gemini. Being inside the Mercury was like being inside a telephone booth. The Gemini was about as roomy as the front seat of a small foreign car. The inside of the Apollo capsule was about as big as the inside of a station wagon.

The cone-shaped capsule was 10 feet 7 inches high and 12 feet 10 inches in diameter at its widest point, which was its blunt end. Its inside was to be a control center, office, kitchen, bedroom, and bathroom for three men for an entire flight, except for the time when two of the men would be in the lunar module for the descent to the moon. The command module's walls were lined with a fantastically complicated instrument panel and consoles, and its cupboards held many kinds of equipment, as well as their food, water, clothing, and waste disposal facilities.

Crewmen would spend most of their time in the three contour couches. The astronaut in the left-hand couch was the spacecraft commander who would usually operate the spacecraft's controls. In the center couch was the command module pilot. He would often work in a well in front of his couch, where he could operate the sextant and telescope for navigation sightings. On the moon trip, he would be the astronaut who would be left behind in the command module while the other two men went to the moon's surface. The astronaut in the right-hand couch was the landing bug's pilot, and his main task would be to check the spacecraft systems—the electricity and oxygen supplies, the fuel system, and the radio and television lines to earth.

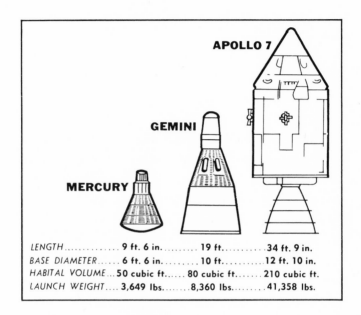

SPACECRAFT COMPARED

APOLLO 7

GEMINI

MERCURY

LENGTH.............. 9 ft. 6 in.......... 19 ft.......... 34 ft. 9 in.
BASE DIAMETER...... 6 ft. 6 in......... 10 ft.......... 12 ft. 10 in.
HABITAL VOLUME...50 cubic ft...... 80 cubic ft....... 210 cubic ft.
LAUNCH WEIGHT....3,649 lbs........8,360 lbs........41,358 lbs.

Apollo was different from Mercury and Gemini in one other way. In Apollo, the astronauts could get up and move around. With the center couch folded, two astronauts could stand at the same time. Two men could sleep in sleeping bags hung hammock-like below the couches.

The command module had five windows: two side windows, two "rendezvous" windows, and a hatch window. The side windows were placed beside the left and the right couches for the purpose of photography and observation. The triangular rendezvous windows, about 8 by 13 inches, were at the ends of the left and right couches. The command module pilot would look through them to steer the module to its rendezvous and link-up with the landing bug.

Toward the narrow end of the cone-shaped module was the tunnel that the two moon-bound astronauts would crawl through to get in and out of the attached landing bug.

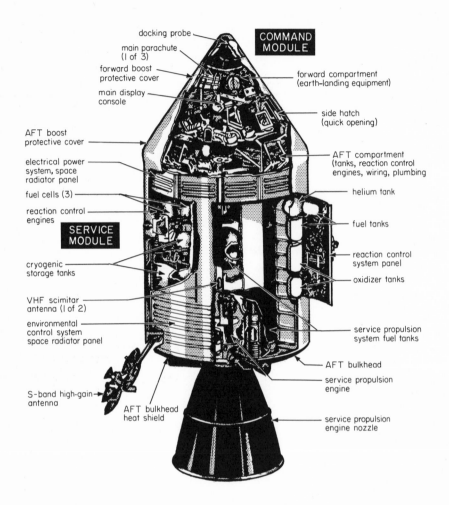

docking probe

main parachute
(1 of 3)

forward boost
protective cover

main display
console

COMMAND
MODULE

forward compartment
(earth-landing equipment)

side hatch
(quick opening)

AFT boost
protective cover

electrical power
system, space
radiator panel

fuel cells (3)

reaction control
engines

SERVICE
MODULE

AFT compartment
(tanks, reaction control
engines, wiring, plumbing

helium tank

fuel tanks

reaction control
system panel

oxidizer tanks

cryogenic
storage tanks

VHF scimitar
antenna (1 of 2)

environmental
control system
space radiator panel

service propulsion
system fuel tanks

AFT bulkhead

service propulsion
engine

S-band high-gain
antenna

AFT bulkhead
heat shield

service propulsion
engine nozzle

SERVICE MODULE

The service module was the section of Apollo beneath the blunt end of the command module. No men would ever ride in it. It would never reach the moon and would be jettisoned just before re-entry to earth. The service module would hold the main rocket for the spacecraft, the rocket fuel, and most of the supplies— oxygen, water, and electrical power units. The service module was

President John F. Kennedy set the course for our space program in 1961 when he announced that the United States would attempt to land men on the moon "before this decade is out." Within less than a year astronaut John H. Glenn, Jr., became the first American to orbit the earth. Astronaut Glenn is shown here after his orbital flight presenting a "hard hat" to the President in an informal ceremony. The hat is a standard piece of safety headgear worn by anyone working around the tall rocket-launch towers of Cape Kennedy.

The original seven Mercury astronauts in their space suits became familiar figures to the nation as the space program developed. These first American spacemen, chosen after exhaustive tests of their stamina and skill, were Alan B. Shepard, Jr., Virgil I. Grissom, L. Gordon Cooper, Walter M. Shirra, Jr., Donald K. Slayton, John H. Glenn, Jr., and M. Scott Carpenter. Because of an unusual heart condition, Slayton was ruled out of space flight but stayed in the program. Grissom was killed in a fire aboard Apollo during ground testing. Carpenter transferred to underwater experimental work after making an orbital flight.

Radar tracking and communications stations were set up around the world to follow the manned space flights. Mission Control Center (bottom photo) was established at the space center in Houston to monitor every action of the rockets, capsules, and astronauts for most of the Gemini and all of the Apollo missions.

Edward H. White was the first American to walk in space. White is shown here against the dramatic backdrop of the earth as he floats outside the orbiting Gemini 4 space ship. White was attached to the space ship by an umbilical cord which provided life support and prevented his drifting away from the ship. The astronaut maneuvered around the ship with the aid of a hand-held gas-firing jet gun. At the right of the picture is the open hatch of the space ship.

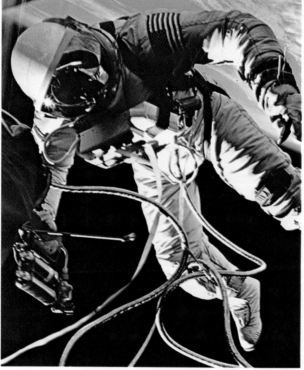

Later Gemini missions further tested space suits outside the capsules, as well as man's ability to perform useful tasks in space.

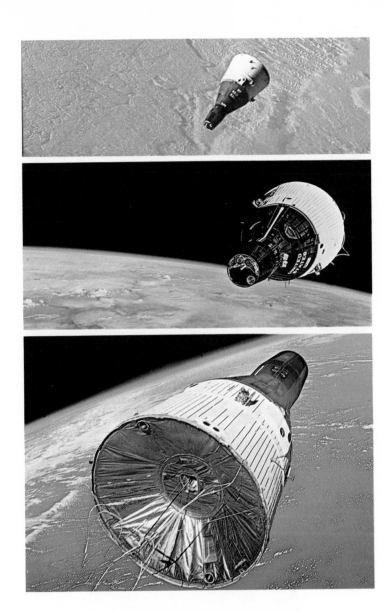

Gemini ships 6 and 7 achieved the first space rendezvous. Gemini 6 pursued Gemini 7 for 100,000 miles at a speed of 17,000 miles per hour until the two ships came within a foot of one another at an orbiting altitude of 185 miles above the earth. The feat was hailed as the most important step after John Glenn's orbital flight.

Eugene Cernan (right) and Thomas Stafford (not pictured) were
scheduled to dock their Gemini 9 with an unmanned Agena, but
the protective shroud of the Agena failed to break free and the
maneuver was not attempted. Stafford described the Agena as
looking like "an angry alligator." Astronaut Charles P. Conrad (left),

accompanied by Richard F. Gordon, achieved the docking maneuver in Gemini 11. They fired the Agena engine to boost their ship into an orbit of 850 miles out from the earth, the farthest man had ventured at that time.

This time exposure of the downward swing of the launch tower shows the action as a Titan rocket blasts off. Titan was the launch vehicle for Gemini flights.

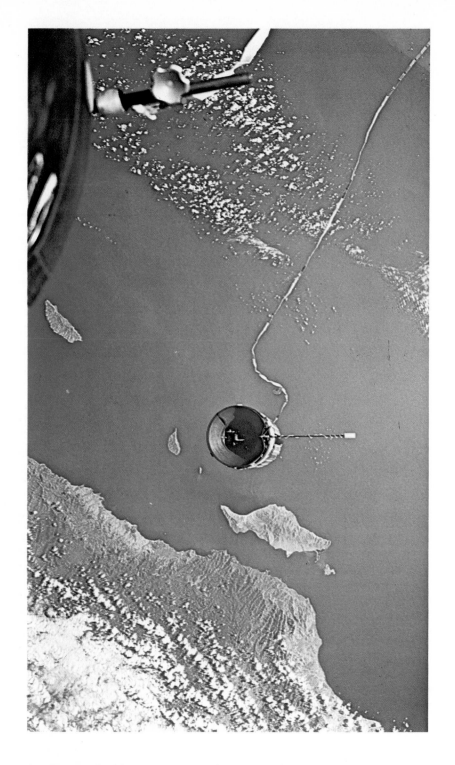

An Agena docking target attached to a Gemini capsule in orbit.

John W. Young smiles up at a recovery helicopter after the successful first flight of Gemini. Young and Virgil I. Grissom put their capsule down in the water, where teams of frogmen attached flotation
collars to insure that the capsule stayed upright and afloat. The astro-

nauts were then hoisted aboard helicopters and flown to waiting recovery ships. On an early Mercury mission with Grissom aboard, a hatch blew open too soon and the capsule sank before rescue teams could secure it. Grissom barely managed to escape.

The first Apollo crew died in a fire aboard the space ship during ground tests January 27, 1967. Virgil I. Grissom was a veteran of both Mercury and Gemini missions. Edward White was the first American to walk in space during the flight of Gemini 4. Roger B. Chaffee was scheduled to make his first flight. The fire apparently started in electrical wiring and swept through the cockpit with furnace-like intensity, fed by the pure oxygen atmosphere inside the spacecraft. An investigation blamed thoughtlessly placed wiring, haphazardly placed combustible materials scattered throughout the cockpit, the pure oxygen the men were breathing, and a cumbersome escape hatch. Modifications and safety precautions made later Apollos much safer, but the program nearly stalled as a result of the tragedy.

Pictures of Langrenus and other craters taken by unmanned satellites and by early Apollo flights were used to determine the best landing sites for the ultimate touchdown on the moon.

Saturn 5 blasts off. The rocket with Apollo spacecraft stands 363 feet high, and its first stage develops 7.5 million pounds of thrust. The second and third stages develop 1,125,000 pounds and 225,000 pounds respectively. The Saturn Apollo is taller than the Statue of Liberty and weighs well over 6 million pounds.

Views of the earth as seen from Apollo 8 as it sped on its way to orbit the moon. Astronauts Frank Borman, James A. Lovell, Jr., and William A. Anders were the first space travelers to watch the earth receding into the distance in just this way. Even at 207,000 miles away the men could identify seas and land masses.

Apollo 9 tested the lunar module in earth orbit and performed rendezvous maneuvers like those which would be used in preparation for the moon landing. Aboard the lunar module were James A. McDivitt and Russell L. Schweickart, while David R. Scott handled the

command module. The photo at top left shows Schweickart outside the LM. The lower left photo is of the lunar module still covered with an aluminum shroud used in the launching phase. At the
right, the legs of the LM are extended and it is ready to descend.

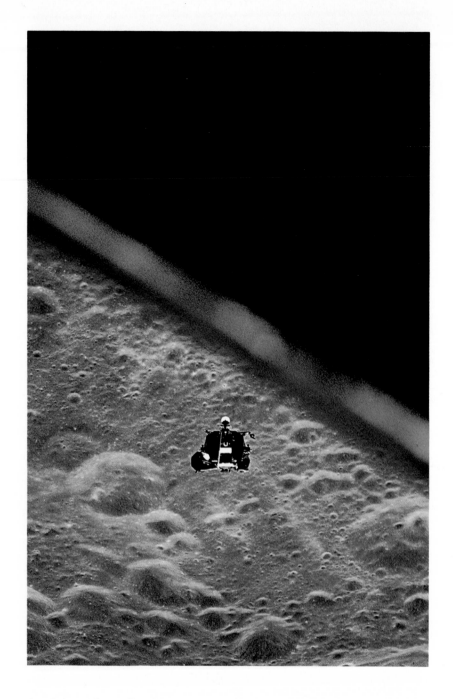

A rainbow-like reflection from within the command ship highlights
this picture of the LM on its way toward the moon in the "near miss"
mission of Apollo 10, flown by Stafford, Cernan, and John W. Young.
In this final mission before the moon landing, Stafford and Cernan
took their LM within 50,000 feet of the lunar surface.

Close-up photographs of ridges and craters on the moon helped establish the lunar landing site.

July 20, 1969, men stand on the surface of the moon. Astronaut Edwin E. Aldrin, Jr., walks on the fine sand of the moon, the life support system on his back and his space suit protecting him from the airless void. He stands near the foil-sheathed landing leg of the LM.

Aldrin plants a solar wind collector to obtain information about emissions from the sun.

Away from the LM, Aldrin sets up the Passive Experiments package, which included a seismometer to record any moon tremors caused by meteorites, volcanic eruptions, or quakes in the moon's surface.

Also included in the experiments was a two-foot square laser reflector which would reflect a beam of light directly back to earth. The travel time of the light beam would indicate subtle changes in earth-moon distances.

Aldrin's face plate reflects a view of the LM and of Neil Armstrong, who took the picture.

Aldrin eases down the ladder to make the last step that will place him on the moon after a four-day journey through space.

Neil A. Armstrong places his foot where no man had walked before.

just as wide as the command module but more than twice as long —24 feet 2 inches. Its relatively simple structure consisted of a center section or tunnel running the length of the cylinder surrounded by six pie-shaped sections. The supplies and electrical power units would be inside these sections.

In the center was the main rocket. It was a restartable engine, with a bell-shaped nozzle jutting out the rear end of the service module, that could blast with a force of 20,500 pounds. This rocket would take the ship into and out of lunar orbit.

LAUNCH ESCAPE SYSTEM

For a short time after lift-off, the Apollo spacecraft would carry a framework tower rising above the command module's nose. This was the 33-foot-high launch escape tower. Its 147,000-pound thrust rocket was ready, on command, to fire and pull the command module away from the rest of the spacecraft and the Saturn 5 in case of serious trouble. The rocket would shoot the command module and the three astronauts out to sea and safety. In the event all went well with the launching, the escape tower would be jettisoned and allowed to fall back into the sea.

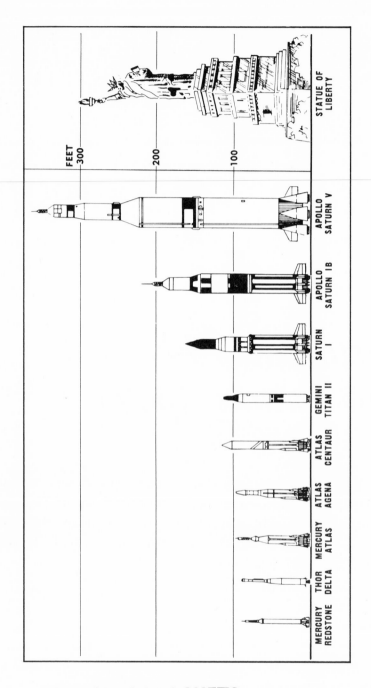

U.S. SPACE ROCKETS
COMPARED

Astronauts Fly
the Saturn-Apollo

The time came, at last, when the Saturn-Apollo was ready for manned flight. Four bold missions were carried out by astronauts as they tested the ship in space between the earth and the moon. These missions were beautiful, precision tests that paved the way for the Apollo 11 moon trip.

APOLLO 7

Apollo 7 was a test of the moonship in an orbit around the earth. The launch date was October 11, 1968. The astronauts were Walter Schirra, Donn F. Eisele, and Walter Cunningham.

The first two days of the mission were crammed with tests of the ship's electrical, navigational, propulsion, and control systems. The Saturn booster had been jettisoned, and was still in orbit. Schirra used the orbiting booster as a target for rendezvous maneuvers. A major objective of the mission was to perform eight firings of the Apollo engine, and all eight went perfectly, sometimes kicking the astronauts into an orbit as high as 277 miles, but always giving them a powerful kick. Once, firing the big 20,500-pound-thrust service module rocket, Schirra exclaimed: "Yaba daba doo! That was a ride and a half."

There were some small problems on board the Apollo 7. One instrument gave a false warning on the ship's oxygen flow. Also, some faulty switches temporarily shut down part of the ship's electrical system. Some of the foods brought complaints from the astronauts as being too sweet, and the water often tasted too much of chlorine. For several days the crew, especially Wally Schirra,

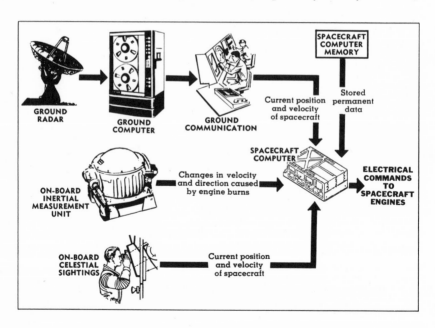

APOLLO GUIDANCE AND CONTROL SYSTEM

battled plain old-fashioned head colds. Schirra had a very bold, independent way of skippering his ship. He canceled the first of Apollo 7's planned telecasts from orbit and several times sharply questioned orders from ground controllers.

But as Apollo 7 settled down to the routine of its long flight, the telecasts came to be highlights of each day. They ran about 7 to 11 minutes as the spacecraft passed over tracking stations at Corpus Christi, Texas, and Cape Kennedy. The *Wally, Walt, and Donn Show,* as it was nicknamed, was the first successful live telecast from American astronauts. The astronauts held up crudely lettered signs that read "Hello from the lovely Apollo Room, high above everything." In these television broadcasts, the world caught some brief, inside glimpses of life aboard an orbiting spacecraft.

After 163 almost flawless orbits of the earth, logging more than 4 million miles and taking hundreds of photographs of earth and the eye of a hurricane, the Apollo 7 astronauts rode their command module down to a splashdown October 22 in the choppy

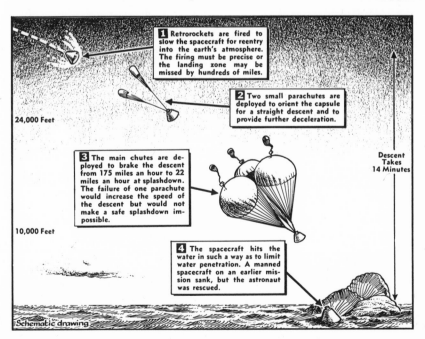

1 Retrorockets are fired to slow the spacecraft for reentry into the earth's atmosphere. The firing must be precise or the landing zone may be missed by hundreds of miles.

2 Two small parachutes are deployed to orient the capsule for a straight descent and to provide further deceleration.

24,000 Feet

3 The main chutes are deployed to brake the descent from 175 miles an hour to 22 miles an hour at splashdown. The failure of one parachute would increase the speed of the descent but would not make a safe splashdown impossible.

Descent Takes 14 Minutes

10,000 Feet

4 The spacecraft hits the water in such a way as to limit water penetration. A manned spacecraft on an earlier mission sank, but the astronaut was rescued.

Schematic drawing

waters south of Bermuda. The swells tipped the spacecraft over, but the crew quickly inflated air bags to right the vehicle so that its apex with the antenna was pointed upward. Soon the astronauts were aboard the recovery ship.

APOLLO 8

Apollo 8 was a test in which an Apollo moonship was put into orbit around the moon. The astronauts who went on this trip were the first men to travel into deep space beyond an earth orbit. They were Frank Borman, James A. Lovell, Jr., and William A. Anders. The launch was on December 21, 1968, shooting the Apollo far out through space and, at last, into orbit around the moon.

As the astronauts came around the eastern edge of the moon, traveling westward near the equator, the sun was shining high overhead. Most of the moon's back side and the eastern edge of the side facing earth were in sunlight. Much of the center part of the moon's face was partly illuminated by earthshine.

One of the first major lunar features the astronauts spotted was Langrenus, one of the many craters with peaks rising from the center of their floors. They next flew over the broad plain called the Sea of Fertility. When asked by ground controllers what "the old moon looks like," Lovell began describing the sights unfolding below:

"The moon is essentially gray, no color. Looks like plaster of paris or sort of grayish beach sand. We can see quite a bit of detail. The Sea of Fertility doesn't stand out as well here as it does back on earth. There's not as much contrast between that and the surrounding craters. The craters are all rounded off. There's quite a few of 'em. Some of them are newer. Many of them look like—especially the round ones—look like they were hit by meteorites or projectiles of some sort. Langrenus is quite a huge crater. It's got a central cone to it. The walls of the craters are terraced, about six or seven different terraces on the way down."

By then Apollo 8 had passed over much of the daytime areas of the moon and was reaching the Sea of Tranquility, an even broader plain on the right side of the moon as seen from earth. With the sun lower, close to the horizon, the astronauts were able to make out more details and their perception of depth and height on the lunar surface was enhanced. This was the way they wanted it. For, on the Sea of Tranquility, lay one of the five sites being considered for the manned lunar landing.

"It's about impossible to miss," Lovell assured the flight controllers. "Very easy to pick out."

The spacecraft then passed over the terminator—the point where daylight changes to darkness. The view in that area, the astronauts reported, was quite sharp. But beyond, even with the earthshine, it became more and more difficult to make out any landmarks.

After moving around the back side and reappearing in their second orbit, the astronauts aimed their $4\frac{1}{2}$-pound television camera toward the moon and transmitted pictures, beginning at 7:29 A.M. It was the first of two television broadcasts from the vicinity of the moon that were seen not only at the Houston control center but in millions of homes throughout the world—wherever people had television sets.

Throughout their orbit, the astronauts gave many of the small, unnamed craters on the back side the names of friends and associates. They even named three for themselves. The craters they named Borman, Lovell, and Anders lie just south of the equator, near where the back of the moon ends and the front begins. Apollo officials said that the crater names were in no way official, merely handy labels to identify some nameless features.

During the telecast, Anders, who handled the camera, described the scene below: "The color of the moon looks like a very whitish gray, like dirty beach sand with lots of footprints in it."

At the end of the second complete orbit, when Apollo 8 was once more behind the moon, its main rocket refired. This dropped the spacecraft from an egg-shaped orbit to a circular orbit nearly 70 miles above the lunar surface.

While orbiting the moon, the astronauts became the first men to witness a lunar sunrise and found it a strange and unexpected experience. According to Lovell, about two minutes before sunrise, a fine white haze appeared over the horizon of the moon, where the sun was about to appear. "It takes a fan shape," he said, "unlike the sunrise on earth, where the atmosphere affects it."

At about 9:30 P.M. on Christmas Eve, the astronauts began their second and last television show from lunar orbit. It ran about 30 minutes and showed the bright moon, in a pitch-black sky, outside the spacecraft window. Borman, describing the moon as a "vast, lonely and forbidding sight," added that it was "not a very inviting place to live or work." Lovell saw the earth as a "grand oasis in the big vastness of space."

As the Christmas Eve telecast neared its end, Borman radioed, "Apollo 8 has a message for you." While the camera showed a view of the craters and mountains of the moon, Anders read the first words from the Book of Genesis:

> In the beginning, God created the heaven and earth.
> And the earth was without form, and void; and darkness was upon the face of the deep . . .

Lovell then took up with the verse beginning,

> And God called the light Day, and the darkness He called Night.

Borman closed the reading with the verse that read:

And God called the dry land Earth, and the gathering together of the waters called He Seas: and God saw that it was good.

After that, Borman signed off, saying:

Good-by, good night. Merry Christmas. God bless all of you, all of you on the good earth.

RETURN TO EARTH

After orbiting the moon 10 times in about 20 hours, Apollo 8 headed back toward earth early Christmas morning. It fired its main rocket engine at 1:10 A.M. to kick out of lunar orbit and begin the 57-hour coasting voyage toward a splashdown in the Pacific Ocean.

Once again, tension had gripped everyone in the control room at Houston. For the rocket firing took place when the spacecraft was directly behind the moon, out of radio contact with earth. If the rocket failed to fire, the astronauts of Apollo 8 would remain in lunar orbit, doomed to die when their oxygen supply ran out. It was about 15 minutes before flight controllers got word that all was well.

Through a distance of 231,000 miles, as Apollo 8 swung around from behind the moon and started for earth, Lovell broadcast the good news, saying these words: "Please be informed there is a Santa Claus." The Apollo rocket on which the astronauts' lives depended had fired perfectly.

The astronauts again went on live television to show how they ate and exercised and how they guided and controlled their 33-foot-long ship. At the time, Apollo 8 was traveling 2,929 miles an hour toward earth, 191,750 miles away.

Inside the cabin, Borman was seated in the commander's

couch at the left side. Anders, the cameraman and systems engineer, was working by his couch at the right side. In the middle, Lovell's couch was folded back and he was lying suspended in a weightless condition in the middle of the cabin. His head was out of sight down in the lower equipment bay. His feet could be seen strapped to a wall to keep him from floating around.

All three astronauts wore their soft strap-on hats, equipped with microphones and earphones. They called them their "Snoopy hats," after the comic-strip beagle who often imagines he is a daring World War I fighter pilot. Instead of the bulky pressure suits worn for the lift-off, they wore the more comfortable flight coveralls made of light-weight Beta cloth, a fire-resistant material. On their feet were soft bootie-like boots.

Lovell moved into the equipment area to demonstrate how the astronauts took their exercise. Lying on his back, he pulled two stretchable cords attached to a well near his feet. "He's working with an exercise device that's designed to keep the muscles in shape," explained Borman, the narrator.

Anders prepared some hot cocoa. He cut a tip of the cocoa bag open with scissors and squirted five ounces of hot water into it with a pistol-like injector. Each squeeze released one-half ounce. Then Anders passed the bag to another astronaut. And for good measure, he handed over bags of sugar cookies, orange drink, corn chowder, chicken and gravy, and "a little napkin to wipe your hands when you're done."

Borman described what Anders was doing to prepare some orange drinks: "You can see he's taking the scissors and cutting the plastic end off the little nozzle that he's going to insert the water gun into. And the water's going in. I hope that you'll have better Christmas dinners today than this."

The astronauts, however, had a better meal than that shown on the telecast. It was a TV dinner of real turkey (not dehydrated), cranberry-apple sauce, and a grape drink.

The next television shot showed Lovell at work down in the lower equipment bay that housed his navigation instruments. These included a sextant and scanning telescope with which the astronauts measured the angles from the spacecraft to different target stars and landmarks on the moon. During the day, Lovell made a number of star sightings. "This is where we find out exactly where we are in space, what direction, and how fast we are traveling," he explained. "And our computer takes the information and tells how to maneuver to get home safely."

On December 26, their last full day in space, the astronauts' thoughts turned more and more to earth. During the afternoon telecast, their last of the mission, Anders mused: "I think I must have the feeling that the travelers in the old sailing ships used to have, going on a very long voyage away from home and now we're headed back. I have that feeling of being proud of the trip but still happy to be going back home." The three men spent most of the day carefully checking out their maneuvering rockets, charging batteries, stowing equipment, and dumping waste water in preparation for their return to earth—considered one of the riskiest phases of the mission. Flight controllers cautioned against talking of a successful mission before it was over.

By the time Apollo 8 had reached the upper layers of the atmosphere at about 400,000 feet, the cylindrical service module had already been separated from the cone-shaped command module in which the astronauts were riding. The bolts holding the two modules together were blown away by the firing of small explosive charges.

Shortly after the service module separation, the on-board computer triggered the firing of six thruster rockets to turn the spacecraft's blunt end toward the line of flight. The men were thus riding down backward.

The outer surface of the command module was coated with a plastic, from a half inch to two inches thick on the blunt end.

This coating was a shield against the heat that built up on the command module's outer surface when it slammed against the atmosphere. The material turned white-hot from the friction, charred, and melted away. But, as it melted, it was doing its job —carrying away tremendous amounts of heat so that the inside of the capsule would not get very hot.

The first of a series of three parachute systems opened automatically 8 minutes after re-entry began, when the spacecraft was 23,300 feet above earth. By then, it had slowed to about 300 miles an hour. First to unfold were the two 14-foot-wide drogue chutes, which oriented the craft and continued slowing it. Less than a minute later, Apollo 8 was dropping straight down. Then three small parachutes pulled out the three main parachutes, each 83 feet in diameter. When the nose broke away to let out the parachutes, it exposed a beacon. This flashing white light could be seen from the aircraft carrier Yorktown and the waiting helicopters as Apollo 8 hit the water at about 20 miles an hour—only 4 miles from the Yorktown.

APOLLO 9

Apollo 8 had orbited the moon. But there had been no test of the four-legged lunar module. In fact, the lunar module had not even been carried along on that mission. Instead, tanks of water had been carried, as ballast, to fill in for the weight of the missing craft.

Now, Apollo 9 would test the lunar module in an earth orbit. The men chosen for the mission were James A. McDivitt, David R. Scott, and Russell L. Schweickart. Their goal would be to maneuver the command module and the lunar module separately in orbit, and to bring them together for rendezvous and docking.

The United States was not the only country planning to carry out rendezvous and docking tests in orbit. On January 14, 1969, while preparations were being made for the Apollo 9 mission, the Soviet Union sent two manned Soyuz spacecraft into earth orbit. One pilot was aboard Soyuz 4, launched on January 14. Three men were on Soyuz 5, launched the following day. The two ships joined each other in space and on January 16, two of the three men from Soyuz 5 "walked" outside to transfer from their craft to Soyuz 4. It was the first time men had transferred from one orbiting vehicle to another.

Several weeks later, at 11 A.M. on March 3, the Apollo 9 astronauts rocketed into space. Within 11 minutes after lift-off, they were in orbit. The first two stages of the Saturn 5 had been jettisoned. Therefore, the ship that was in orbit had these parts, beginning at the tail end:

1. The third stage of Saturn 5
2. The Lunar Module, mounted inside a metal casing attached to the Saturn front end
3. The Service Module, including the Apollo rocket engine, just forward of the lunar module
4. The cone-shaped Command Module at the forward end of the ship

The ship was arranged in this way because the command module (where the three astronauts were) had a sleek, streamlined shape that made it a good front end for the launch through the air. But now, out in space, the lunar module had to be moved to the front. It could not be left in back because it would be in the way of the Apollo rocket when it began to blast.

To change the line-up, the two halves of the ship were separated. The service module and command module moved forward, leaving the Saturn third stage and the lunar module behind for the time being. Then Scott turned the command ship through a backward flip and gingerly pulsed small rockets to move 50 feet back for a nose-to-nose link-up with the landing module, still attached to the Saturn.

On the moon landing mission, the Saturn third stage would be used to boost the Apollo out of its earth orbit toward the moon. But, for this test, Apollo was not going to the moon. So, instead, Scott flipped a switch that jettisoned the Saturn third stage in earth orbit. Then, from the ground control center, a signal went to the Saturn computer that made the jettisoned third stage blast far off into an orbit around the sun. The astronauts had maneuvered their craft several thousand feet away by then and could watch the Saturn's spectacular rocket flame. Scott radioed: "It's just like a bright star disappearing in the distance."

After the jettison, all that was left were the three modules of the Apollo. At the back of the command module was the rocket-carrying service module. Together, they formed the main part of the spaceship. Attached to the nose end of this ship was the strange-looking lunar module. A connecting tunnel went between the service module and the lunar module. At each end of the tunnel was a hatch.

On the third day, March 5, the astronauts used that tunnel. Slowed down by bulky, partially inflated spacesuits and oxygen hoses, they removed the command module hatch and reached through the connecting tunnel to open the lunar module hatch. Then Schweickart and later McDivitt crawled through the tunnel (38 inches long and 32 inches wide) into the lunar module. The two men spent nearly 9 hours there, while Scott remained to pilot the command ship. McDivitt and Schweickart switched on nearly all of the lunar module's instruments, extended its four spindly legs, sampled its computer data to make sure it was working well, and ignited the descent engine for a 6-minute firing. They also sent out a short telecast of their activities inside the lunar module cockpit.

The landing module was declared in good shape—which was more than could be said for Schweickart at the time. Twice during these activities, he was hit by severe attacks of nausea, perhaps a form of motion sickness. For a time, flight controllers canceled plans to have Schweickart take a 2-hour space "walk"—called extravehicular activity, or EVA. Though not a high-priority part of the mission, EVA was included to give the astronauts training in the emergency procedure for moving from one vehicle to another if something should block passage through the tunnel or if, on the return from the moon, the two ships were unable to link up when they rendezvoused. It would also provide the first real test of the oxygen-supplying backpack men would use while walking on the moon's surface.

When the astronauts awoke the next day—March 6, their fourth day in orbit—Schweickart had recovered from his nausea and was ready to go EVA in open space.

McDivitt and Schweickart, who had returned to the command module for the night, went back through the tunnel into the lunar module. All three astronauts were fully suited, breathing oxygen piped directly into their suits. The oxygen was let out of both cabins, so that the insides of the modules were complete vacuums, just like the surrounding space. Then hatches on both modules were opened.

Scott stuck his head and shoulders out of the command module hatch to pick up some experiments that had been attached outside. As Apollo 9 soared over the Pacific Ocean at sunrise, Schweickart stepped out on the lunar module's porch-like platform. He spent most of his 40-minute EVA with his booted feet securely planted in a pair of "golden slippers" attached to the porch. These were hard-rubber foot anchors that were covered with gold paint as protection against the sun's intense rays. Being anchored in this way—a lesson learned from the Gemini EVA's—Schweickart could use both hands to operate cameras. "That's what you call a view from the top of the stairs—one stair, that is," Schweickart said.

After Schweickart's EVA, the astronauts shut the hatches and returned to the command module to rest up for their fifth and most critical day in orbit—the day of rendezvous. The rendezvous maneuver was a spectacular display of navigation that lasted for about 6½ hours. McDivitt and Schweickart went back into the lunar module and, when all was ready on Apollo's 59th orbit around the earth, Scott tripped a switch in the command module cockpit to release the twelve latches holding the two ships together at the tunnel.

"Spider" was then free of "Gumdrop." In their radio communications between the two ships, the astronauts referred to the lunar module as Spider, because of its insect-like appearance, and to the command module as Gumdrop, because the cone-shaped vehicle was delivered from the factory to the Cape in a blue, plastic, candy-like wrapping.

After making sure that Spider was working perfectly, McDivitt and Schweickart fired small lunar module rockets to pull their ship away from Scott and Gumdrop. For an hour they drifted within a few miles of Gumdrop, checking out their rendezvous radar and guidance systems. Then McDivitt fired up the lunar module's descent rocket to climb into a 156-mile-high orbit, 13 miles above the command module. "It got a little rough and shaky as I was throttling up," McDivitt reported. The lunar module continued on its course for nearly two hours while the two craft circled the earth, their maximum distance from each other reaching 50 miles.

Then when Spider got back within sight of Gumdrop, McDivitt refired the descent rocket. Shortly afterward, he triggered explosive bolts to jettison the lunar module's lower stage with its four legs, exposing the nozzle of their ascent rocket. When the lunar module, flying higher in an "outside track," fell behind about 100 miles, McDivitt fired the ascent engine the way it would be done at take-off from the moon. With several firings, McDivitt and Schweickart steadily closed the gap between themselves and Gumdrop. If they had failed to find Gumdrop, the two men in Spider would have been stranded in orbit to die when their oxygen supply ran out.

But their radar and rockets worked flawlessly. When the squat, bug-like lunar module hove into view, Scott radioed greetings: "You're the biggest, friendliest, funniest-looking spider I've ever seen."

Finally, coached by Scott, McDivitt slowly brought the lunar module up to the mother ship for the redocking. After McDivitt and Schweickart squeezed back through the tunnel into the command module, the astronauts released the lunar module, and, on a radioed command from the ground, the ascent engine was refired until all of its fuel was gone. Both the descent and ascent stages of the lunar module were now only so much space junk which would burn up as they dipped back into earth's atmosphere several weeks later.

After completing the rendezvous, the Apollo 9 astronauts were left alone in orbit with fully 97 per cent of their mission objectives already completed, but with five more days of flight. They made good use of the time, practicing navigation and tracking skills and conducting photographic experiments designed to study the earth. On March 13, the three astronauts brought their spacecraft to a smooth and accurate splashdown in the Atlantic Ocean north of Puerto Rico. It hit the water less than a mile away from its target point and only three miles north of the waiting recovery ship, the U.S.S. Guadalcanal. Television cameras on the helicopter carrier were able to show the worldwide audience the last moments of the parachute-aided descent and all of the recovery operations by helicopter and frogmen. The men were safe and healthy after ten successful days in space.

APOLLO 10

In May, 1969, the Apollo 10 was launched. Apollo 8 had carried out a moon orbit without taking along the lunar module. Apollo 9 had tested the lunar module, but did not leave earth orbit. Apollo 10 was to combine both of these missions. The astronauts' job was to take the Apollo into a lunar orbit *and* to test the lunar module. They would do everything except make a moon landing. This mission would be the final practice for the Apollo 11 moon trip.

The astronauts chosen for Apollo 10 were Thomas P. Stafford, John W. Young, and Eugene A. Cernan. The three men named their round-ended command module "Charlie Brown," and they named their four-legged lunar module "Snoopy."

A perfect launching sent the three astronauts on their moonward course early on a Sunday afternoon. After circling the earth one and a half times, the Saturn 5's third-stage engine refired for 5 minutes to blast the spaceship out of its low earth orbit at a speed of about 24,200 miles an hour. "We're on the way!" radioed Stafford.

In a maneuver just like the one done for Apollo 9, the astronauts separated their command module from the rest of the "stack," did a back flip, and moved its nose in for a docking with the lunar module, nestled on top of the Saturn 5 third stage. Then, while their color television camera was transmitting, the astronauts pulled the attached lunar module out of its nest and watched the Saturn 5 drop back in the blackness of space.

For three days Apollo 10 and its crew coasted toward the moon, losing speed until, within 38,000 miles of the moon, they were pulled ever faster by the moon's gravity. It was a relaxed time. Some of the problems of the earlier flights, the colds and nausea, were missing. The astronauts' only complaints were too much chlorine in the water, hydrogen bubbles in the water that caused stomach gas, and some drifting snow-like particles of glass fiber from a rip in the command module's hatch covering.

At 4:45 P.M., Eastern Daylight Time, on May 21, Apollo 10's service module rocket fired to slow down the ship and send the astronauts into an orbit of the moon. The astronauts then turned their color television camera on, to give the people back home a 29-minute show of what it was like to fly over the craters of the moon.

Early the next morning, Cernan and Stafford crawled through the connecting tunnel into Snoopy, leaving Young behind in Charlie Brown. After checking all instruments, the two astronauts separated their lunar module from the command module. Then, firing the lunar module's descent rocket, they streaked down through the lunar sky at a speed of 3,700 miles an hour. "We're right there! We're right over it," Cernan called over his radio. "I'm telling you, we are low, we're close, babe. This is it." Snoopy was soaring 47,000 feet above the moon—not much higher than the altitude at which jet airliners fly over the earth.

On Snoopy's first low pass, Stafford looked out the window and described the Apollo landing site in the Sea of Tranquility. He said that it looked "very smooth, like wet clay, like a dry river bed in New Mexico or Arizona." He was able to pick out many details—boulders, small craters, and deep cracks in the moon's surface.

Just before the second fly-over, the two astronauts in Snoopy had a scare. Explosive bolts were automatically triggered to jettison Snoopy's lower stage with its four spindly legs. At that moment the upper stage went into a fast spin, pitching up and down. "Something is wrong with the gyro," shouted Cernan. Stafford took over the hand controls, and after about a minute was able to steady the spacecraft.

Later, NASA engineers decided that a control switch had been left in the wrong position. That mistake had probably been made before the launch, while the lunar module was being checked out.

By the time Snoopy and its pilots had settled down, they were again within 9 miles of the moon. "I'll tell you," Cernan said, "we're down there where we can touch the top of some of the hills." At this time, the lunar module's rocket fired for 15 seconds to boost the two astronauts back toward their rendezvous with the command module. The rocket sent them on an upward curving course like the one astronauts taking off from the moon would follow. As the two spacecraft docked together, one of the astronauts shouted, "Snoopy and Charlie Brown are hugging each other."

After Stafford and Cernan crawled back into Charlie Brown, they closed the hatches and jettisoned the unmanned lunar module upper stage. Its rocket was fired until all the fuel was burned, sending the craft out into a wide orbit of the moon. Cernan said, "That little Snoopy was a real winner."

To hear Stafford describe it, a ride in the lunar module's upper stage was quite an experience. When the smaller rockets were fired for the last seconds of the rendezvous, he said the thin aluminum alloy walls of the vehicle shook and rattled. "If you wanted a Lunar Module . . . ride," Stafford told ground controllers, "let your kids get a big metal bowl on your head and beat on it with spoons."

The Apollo 10 astronauts kept orbiting the moon for another full day. From their orbit, ranging from altitudes of 63 to 75 miles above the moon, they observed craters that looked like volcanoes and others that looked as if they had been caused by meteor collisions. "There's one on the back side," Stafford said, "that if it was in a different setting you would call it Mount Fujiyama." Later, Stafford reported seeing a crater whose outside slope was covered with "so many big, black boulders" that it looked "like a forest of pine trees."

With a powerful push from their spacecraft rocket, the Apollo 10 astronauts broke out of moon orbit early Saturday morning, May 24, and headed for earth with ever-increasing speed. Their aim was true. Their spacecraft was still performing smoothly. They were tired but in good spirits after their 31 orbits around the moon.

Looking back on the scarred face of the moon, Cernan said: "I tell you, this satellite of ours—this moon of ours—had a rough beginning somewhere back there."

Then Apollo 10 went through the same maneuvers that Apollo 8 followed to get back to earth. The service module was jettisoned. An automatic command from the computer fired maneuvering rockets to point the blunt end of the cone-shaped command module toward the earth at an angle. Then, came the fiery re-entry through the air. Finally, the parachutes unfurled and, as dawn came to the South Pacific, Apollo 10 dropped into the water within sight of the U.S.S. Princeton, a helicopter carrier standing by for the recovery.

CHAPTER 9

Men
for the Moon

"When ships to sail the void between the stars have been in-vented," said Johannes Kepler, the German scientist who had so much to do with explaining the motions of bodies in space, "there will also be men who come forward to sail those ships."

The ships have been invented, and out of the $3\frac{1}{2}$ billion people in the world, the 202 million Americans, and the 50 active astronauts, three men were selected to make the first voyage to land on the moon. They had worked together as a team for more than a year. First, as the backup pilots for Apollo 8, they learned through ground training and long textbook study the ways of a Saturn 5 in flight, of a command module on the way to the moon, and of a fiery re-entry to splashdown. Then, since January, 1969, when they were chosen for Apollo 11, they had practiced for weeks on end at the controls of the command module and the lunar module. The two men who would actually land on the moon spent hours learning geology and photography and studying lunar maps to be able to make the most of the short time they would spend on the moon's surface.

What kind of men are these three astronauts who were chosen for the moon trip?

The commander of the Apollo moonship was Neil Armstrong, blond-haired and boyish looking. This modest, somewhat shy man has had a brave and adventurous flying history. As a Navy pilot he flew 78 combat missions off the carrier Essex in the Korean war. On one of these missions, a cable stretched across a North Korean valley sliced off one wing of his jet. He nursed the plane back over friendly territory and bailed out safely. After the Korean war, he continued his college education, getting a degree in aeronautical engineering from Purdue University. More recently, he has flown many missions in the high-speed X-15 experimental plane as a test pilot, and had several close calls.

Neil Armstrong was born on August 5, 1930, in the living room of his grandparents' farmhouse, six miles from the small town of Wapakoneta, Ohio. His love for flying came early in his life. When he was six, he went for a plane ride with his father in a Ford Tri-Motor. The next year, he began to build model airplanes, a hobby that went on for many years. His feelings about flying also showed up in his dreams. In those years, he would often have a dream in which, by holding his breath, he could rise up into the air and hover above the ground.

As a teenager, Armstrong advanced quickly in school, doing especially well in science and math. In high school, he even substituted for his science teacher when the teacher was out ill for a while. His success in school was not all that he was accomplishing —he took flying lessons, and had his pilot's license before he got his driver's license. He worked as a mechanic at an airport, spent time star-gazing through a neighbor's telescope, and built a wind tunnel in the basement of his parents' home in order to test the wing and body shapes of model airplanes. Aviation and outer space fascinated him.

Throughout all his years of flying adventures, Neil Armstrong has remained a quiet, thoughtful man with a dry sense of humor. His preferred way of life is shown by the fact that he and his wife raised their children in a former forest ranger's cabin in the foothills of the San Gabriel Mountains, instead of living in the nearby town of Lancaster, California, where most of the X-15 test pilots lived.

Edwin E. Aldrin, Jr., who goes by the nickname of "Buzz," was the pilot of the Apollo Lunar Module. Buzz Aldrin is a determined man with a very definite manner. He always knows what his goals are and he knows how to go about reaching them. He is a rugged-looking man, his blond hair mostly gone now, who lives vigorously. He goes in for physical exercise and for staying in good condition, and stays in shape by pole vaulting in his back yard.

Aldrin also flew combat missions in the Korean War. In his 66 missions, flying an F-86 Sabrejet, he shot down two MIG 15's and damaged another.

Buzz Aldrin was born January 20, 1930, in Montclair, New Jersey. His father, Colonel Edwin Eugene Aldrin, Sr., was himself an adventurous flyer, steeped in aviation. The father of the future astronaut studied under Robert Goddard, the rocket pioneer, knew one of the Wright brothers who flew the world's first airplane, and he himself set a cross-country flying record in 1929, the year before Buzz was born.

Buzz Aldrin not only inherited his father's love of flying— he also was strongly successful in his studies. He graduated third highest in his class at West Point and later earned a doctor's degree in astronautics at the Massachusetts Institute of Technology. It has been said that he is the best scientific mind that we have sent into space.

Michael Collins was the pilot of the Command Module. Collins, a former Edwards Airforce Base test pilot, is a dark-haired, relaxed man who likes to raise roses in his backyard and who plays a strong game of handball. He is casual and breezy in his manner, a man who shows his feelings openly, and doesn't take himself too seriously.

Mike Collins was born in Rome, Italy, on October 31, 1930. His father, a United States Army general, was stationed in Rome at the time as a military observer. Mike was an active boy, who enjoyed life a great deal, and who was a good athlete. In his teens, he was captain of the wrestling team at St. Albans School for Boys in Washington, D.C. Then, as now, he was warm, popular, and full of spirit.

Mike went to college at West Point, where he graduated in 1952. His grades there had not been especially good. But he had done well enough, even with his relaxed kind of studying, to get his college degree. Next, he joined the Air Force, where he entered test-pilot school. That was the start of the career that led him, finally, to the Apollo 11 launch pad.

These, then, were the three men who took Apollo to the moon. They have many things in common. All are married men with children. All three had already gone into space on Gemini missions. They were the best kind of men that could be found anywhere for this voyage.

CHAPTER 10

Days
of Waiting

Throughout the history of exploration there had never been an expedition planned and prepared with such care as Apollo 11.

The many and highly complex components of the command module, the lunar module, and the Saturn 5 had been tested in a variety of ways, both on the ground and in space. For years men and computers had worked out the mathematics, plotted the course, and studied the risks. Their work had led to ways to keep the spacecraft from getting too hot or too cold, keep it from losing communications with earth, keep its engines from firing too long or too short, and to stay on course at distances of 250,000 miles from its home base. Such careful preparations continued right through those final days of waiting, the days leading up to launching time on July 16.

Early on June 27, launching crews began the Countdown Demonstration Test (CDDT), or the dress rehearsal, for Apollo 11. This included all the steps of the actual countdown, all the tests, the complete fueling of the rocket, the entrance of the astronauts into the spacecraft cabin. A week later, shortly before 9:32 A.M. on July 3, a clear voice came through the intercom at the Firing Room 1: "You're cleared for firing command." In a few seconds, a man wearing a short-sleeved shirt leaned over his control console and pressed the button that initiated the automatic, 3 minute and 7 second sequence of computerized events leading up to lift-off. Without a hitch, the countdown ticked away to the point of ignition. But it was only a make-believe countdown, the final practice for the real thing.

They were practicing for the mission in a dummy model of the Apollo command module, called a simulator. All the dials and gauges, switches, hand controls and computer display panels were just as they are in the real spacecraft.

For nearly eight hours, while instructors operated the four computers that ran the simulator, the astronauts practiced over and over again the first 12 minutes of the flight. There were times when the make-believe lift-off was free of trouble. Other times, to test the astronauts' reflexes and knowledge of the systems and alternate mission plans, the instructors ordered the computers to throw in an error or two.

For the last two months before the flight, each of the astronauts spent more than 400 hours in command module and lunar module simulators at Cape Kennedy and at Houston. It was thus possible to practice every step of the 8-day mission—launching, earth-orbit operations, the rocket firing to leave low earth orbit and head for the moon, the insertion into lunar orbit, the landing on the moon, the lift-off from the moon and, the return to earth.

One of the most unusual simulators, was a real flying vehicle, the lunar landing traning vehicle. It had a nickname—the "Flying Bedstead." But it had much the same pilot-handling characteristics as the lunar module. Undisturbed by an accident earlier in the year, in which Armstrong had to bail out of a crashing trainer, the two moon explorers spent hours piloting the vehicle to soft touchdowns.

All three astronauts also spent long hours learning their mission plan, operating the guidance and navigation computer (which took nearly 40 per cent of their training time), working in a large vacuum chamber at Houston and getting brief sensations of weightlessness during sudden dips in a KC-135 airplane. But in the last few days before lift-off, the three men slowed down their training. They were following their doctors orders. Having in mind the fatigue and illness that delayed Apollo 9 by three days, Charles A. Berry, the astronauts' flight surgeon, ordered the training slowdown and also placed the crew in semi-quarantine for the final two weeks. The men were watched for the slightest symptoms of illness that might hamper the flight. The only people who could come in contact with them were their training associates and their immediate families—so long as they were healthy.

No exceptions could be made even for the President of the United States. After the arrangements were already made for President Nixon to dine with the astronauts on the night before the launch, Berry "suggested" to the White House that, from a medical standpoint, even the President should not be near the astronauts. The dinner was canceled.

Just as the astronauts were waiting for their moon journey, the possibility of "back-contamination" was dramatized in a chilling best-seller, *The Andromeda Strain.* The book was a fictional story about a strain of alien germs brought back to earth from outer space.

The Apollo 11 astronauts were not likely, however, to bring

back some deadly strain. Biologists doubted that the airless moon had any germs or viruses on it. But, early in the Apollo Project, a committee of the National Academy of Sciences had decided that a strict quarantine was a good idea—just in case. This led to NASA's construction of a laboratory with vacuum chambers for the lunar dirt samples and sealed quarters for the astronauts and their doctors, technicians, and cook. That way, even if there were dangerous moon germs, they would not be easily spread around the earth.

Whatever germs the astronauts brought back from the moon, they were not starting their voyage with any signs of illness. On Friday, July 11, they went through a 4-hour medical examination and were pronounced physically fit for flight.

COUNTDOWN

No magic button was pressed, or switch flipped. A master clock in Firing Room 1 simply began ticking at 8 P.M. on Thursday, July 10. As the clock ticked, launching controllers began sending electrical power to the 363-foot-tall moon vehicle at the pad. It was the beginning of the countdown. The days of waiting were now being measured in hours and minutes and seconds.

"WILLING AND READY"

The countdown proceeded smoothly. Rocco Petrone, the launch director, called it the smoothest yet. The crowds at Cocoa Beach waiting to see the launch grew larger. It was hard to believe but it was happening: men were poised to go to the moon.

Two nights before the launching, Armstrong, Aldrin, and Collins made their final public appearances in a nationally televised 30-minute interview. They were asked questions by four newsmen selected from the 3,000 there. Because of the semi-quarantine, the interview was conducted over closed-circuit television. The astronauts, wearing short-sleeved shirts and sitting in soft chairs, were in one building and the newsmen were 15 miles away in another.

Armstrong appeared slightly nervous, choosing his words with care, and Aldrin was stiff and unsmiling. Only Collins appeared relaxed.

Asked if they had any fears about the mission, Armstrong replied: "Fear is not an unknown emotion to us. But we have no fear of launching out on this expedition."

Aldrin told the newsmen that it was all right to use the term "when" and not "if" in referring to the moon landing. "We're thinking positively," he said.

"After a decade of planning and hard work," Armstrong declared, "we're willing and ready to attempt to achieve our national goal."

CHAPTER 11

Four Days to the Moon

"Go, baby, go!" The familiar murmur spread like fire through the control rooms. Only this time they said it with more feeling than usual. On the beaches, they shaded their eyes against the bright sun and held their breaths. Across the land, they paused at their jobs and rushed to television sets.

This was the "big one" at last. It was not just another space flight. This was *the* historic flight to put men on the moon! Could Armstrong and Aldrin really land and walk on the moon? The whole world waited anxiously to find out.

It was July 16, 1969, and the "big one" began on schedule. At 9:32 A.M., E.D.T., orange flames and dark smoke spewed out of the huge Saturn 5 rocket supporting the Apollo 11 spaceship at Cape Kennedy. Then, ever so slowly, the 3,817-ton vehicle struggled to overcome the earth's gravity, finally cleared the Pad 39-A launching tower, and arced out over the Atlantic Ocean.

As the rocket launched Neil Armstrong, Buzz Aldrin, and Mike Collins on their 8-day, 500,000-mile journey, the powerful blast-off made the ground shake. The Apollo 11 streaked upward through a wispy white cloud, in a trail of fire.

President Nixon, who had watched the lift-off on television in Washington, declared a National Day of Participation for the lunar exploration set for four days hence. Urging that Americans be given the day off from work, he said:

"In past ages, exploration was a lonely enterprise. But today, the miracles of space travel are matched by miracles of space communications; even across the vast lunar distance, television brings the moment of discovery into our homes and makes all of us participants. As the astronauts go where man has never gone, as they attempt what man has never tried, we on earth will want, as one people, to be with them in spirit, to share the glory and the wonder and to support them with prayers that all will go well."

And, certainly all Americans, indeed all mankind, felt that they were a part of this history-in-the-making. The astronauts already were carrying with them tokens to be left on the moon. In addition to the metal plaque attached to a leg of the lunar module, the tokens included messages of goodwill from 73 heads of state, a United States flag, and medals honoring the Soviet cosmonauts and American astronauts who have died in the conquest of space.

Actually, for the first four days of the Apollo journey, the world saw little that was new. Moving toward the moon, the three astronauts closely followed a trail already blazed by Apollo 10 two months before. Until the landing craft with Armstrong and Aldrin aboard swooped to within 50,000 feet of the moon where the final descent began, the crew faced challenges and risks that were familiar. They met with no troubles.

During this time, the astronauts performed the routine tasks of a space flight, checking equipment and systems, carrying out everyday housekeeping chores, and conducting regularly scheduled telecasts for the folks back home. From all indications, the men were comfortable and relaxed. "We have a happy home," Collins said during one of the telecasts. "Plenty of room for the three of us. We're all finding our favorite little corners."

On Friday, when Apollo 11 was three-quarters of the way to the moon, Armstrong and Aldrin took a televised inspection tour of the attached lunar module. To do this, they had to open the hatch of the cone-shaped command ship, Columbia, and then squeeze through the 30-inch-wide tunnel into the lunar module, the Eagle. This was the procedure they were to follow later for the actual descent. The telecast, which ran an hour and 36 minutes, was one of the clearest color TV transmissions ever sent from space. Viewers on earth could read dials on the lunar module control panels.

INTO LUNAR ORBIT

The first really anxious moments of the Apollo mission came around noon on Saturday when the linked Columbia and Eagle swung around the leading edge of the moon to begin the transition into lunar orbit. For 33 minutes, the spacecraft was out of radio contact with tracking stations on earth. During that time, the astronauts had to fire the craft's main rocket to slow the vehicle down so that it could be captured by lunar gravity. If the rocket failed to fire, Apollo 11 would loop the moon and head back to earth. If it fired too long, the vehicle could crash into the lunar surface.

But the rocket performed almost flawlessly. When the spaceship swept into moon orbit, Armstrong broke the tense silence at last: "It was like perfect," he reported.

But everything up to now was really only warm-up for the highly complex descent of Eagle to the lunar surface—the encounter with the unknown. Here was a challenge which men had never tackled before. During a time of little more than 10 minutes, Armstrong and Aldrin had to sweep about 300 miles across the face of the moon in their lunar module, descending on a long curve from 50,000 feet to touchdown. A major equipment failure or a miscalculation could mean turning back from the goal or, in the final phase, disaster. If one of the landing craft's spindly legs broke upon landing because of boulders or an unexpected movement, or if the touchdown happened on a steep slope, the craft could tip over and the astronauts would be unable to lift off for a return trip.

The descent procedure began on the Apollo's thirteenth moon orbit after Armstrong and Aldrin had crawled into the lunar module, leaving Collins to fly the command module. The two ships broke their link and drew apart. "How does it look?" Mission Control asked Armstrong. "Eagle has wings," he replied.

Armstrong and Aldrin rode the Eagle back around to the moon's far side where the descent engine was to fire in order to send the module toward the moon on a long, curving course. Suspense built up in the control room at Houston because once again the astronauts were out of radio touch with the ground.

Armstrong finally broke the suspense with a calm report: "The burn was on time." In the command module, Collins reported to Mission Control, "Listen, baby, things are going just swimmingly, just beautiful."

When Armstrong and Aldrin reached 50,000 feet from the moon's surface, green lights on the computer display keyboard blinked the number 99. This signaled Armstrong that he had 5 seconds to decide whether to go ahead for the landing or return to the command module. The ship commander pressed the "proceed" button.

The engine built up thrust gradually, firing as the lunar module headed toward the moon. Seven minutes after the firing, the astronauts, riding upside down according to flight plan, were 21,000 feet above the surface and moving toward the landing site. The guidance computer was driving the rocket engine. At 7,200 feet, with the landing site about 5 miles ahead, the computer ordered maneuvers to tilt the bug-shaped craft almost upright. Armstrong and Aldrin then got their first close-up view of the plain they were aiming for.

The brownish-gray land rushed below them—the craters, hills, and ridges, deep cracks and ancient rubble of the moon. Their target was in the Sea of Tranquility, one of five smooth landing sites that had been selected along the lunar equator on the basis of pictures taken by unmanned spacecraft. Being on the equator reduces the maneuvering required for the astronauts to get there. The sites were on the side of the moon always facing earth; this, of course, made it possible to communicate with the explorers.

The Eagle closed in on the target, dropping about 20 feet a second until it was hovering almost directly over the selected landing spot at an altitude of 500 feet. Then came a startling blow: the floor was littered with boulders. Armstrong quickly grabbed manual control. As he said later, "The auto-targeting was taking us right into a football-field-sized crater, with a large number of boulders and rocks."

Armstrong retained partial control of the module for the rest of the way down. The computer controlled the rocket firing, but the astronaut could adjust the craft's hovering position. For about 90 seconds, Armstrong searched for a clear spot; finally he found one that he liked. Slowly the craft eased down until a blue light on the cockpit flashed to signal that 5-foot-long probes, like curb feelers, on the legs had touched the surface.

"Houston, Tranquility Base here. The Eagle has landed."

"Roger, Tranquility," ground control replied. "We copy you on the ground. You got a bunch of guys about to turn blue. We are breathing again. Thanks a lot."

Although Armstrong is known as a man of few words, his heartbeats told of his excitement upon leading man's first landing on the moon. At the time of the descent rocket ignition, his heartbeat rate registered 110 a minute—77 is normal for him—and it shot up to 156 at touchdown.

The landing actually was 4 miles down range—meaning 4 miles too far to the west—but it was well within the planned area. When they landed, the astronauts were not sure exactly where they were.

Mission Control immediately reported the landing to Collins, who was riding the command ship Columbia about 65 miles overhead. 'Yea, I heard the whole thing," replied the man who went so far but not all the way. "Fantastic."

Yes, fantastic! They had done it! By flying their craft to the lunar surface and landing there, by conquering this great unknown, Armstrong and Aldrin had proved that the moon was now within man's reach. The next step, the true purpose of this fantastic mission, was to sample the unknown, to walk on the moon and learn how safe or unsafe it was for man.

CHAPTER 12

On the Moon

At 10:56 P.M., E.D.T., on July 20, 1969, Neil A. Armstrong stepped into history. From the bottom rung of the ladder leading down from Apollo 11's landing craft, he reached out his booted left foot and planted the first human footprint on the moon.

Then he said the long-awaited words that are sure to be written in history books: "That's one small step for a man, one giant leap for mankind."

There it was, man meeting moon. For explorers, it was the realization of centuries of dreams. For scientists, it meant a chance for possible clues to the origin and nature of both the moon and the earth.

Armstrong was able to share the triumphal moment with mankind. Through the miracle of modern communications, hundreds of millions of people on earth—probably the largest audience ever —witnessed the astronaut's first step over TV and heard his words on radio. It took just 1.3 seconds, the time it takes for radio waves to travel the 238,000 miles between moon and earth, for Armstrong's image to appear on home screens. This gave viewers a feeling of "I was there" when history was made.

What was this new world like, this remote space frontier suddenly invaded by man? Earlier, looking through the windows of the landing craft, Armstrong and his crewmate, Buzz Aldrin, radioed this first impression of the general area in which they touched down:

> [There is a] level plain cratered with a fairly large number of craters of the 5- to 50-foot variety. And some ridges, small, 20 to 30 feet high, I would guess. And literally thousands of little one- and two-foot craters around the area. We see some angular blocks out several hundred feet in front of us that are probably two feet in size and have angular edges. There is a hill in view just about on the ground track ahead of us. Difficult to estimate, but might be half a mile or a mile . . . I'd say the color of the local surface is very comparable to that we observed from orbit at this sun angle—about 10 degrees sun angle or that nature. It's pretty much without color. It's gray and it's very white as you look into the zero phase line. And it's considerably darker gray, more like an ashen gray, as you look out 90 degrees to the sun. Some of the surface rocks in close here that have been fractured or disturbed by the rocket engine plume are coated with this light gray on the outside. But where they've been broken, they display a dark, very dark, gray interior and it looks like it could be country basalt.

When Armstrong reached the bottom of the lunar module's ladder, he said: "The surface is fine and powdery. I can pick it up loosely with my toe. It does adhere in fine layers like powdered charcoal to the sole and sides of my boots. I only go in a small fraction of an inch, maybe an eighth of an inch. But I can see the footprints of my boots and the treads in the fine sandy particles."

Then, while the excited audience watched those first few moments in awe, Armstrong began to walk carefully across the

LIFE SUPPORT SYSTEM

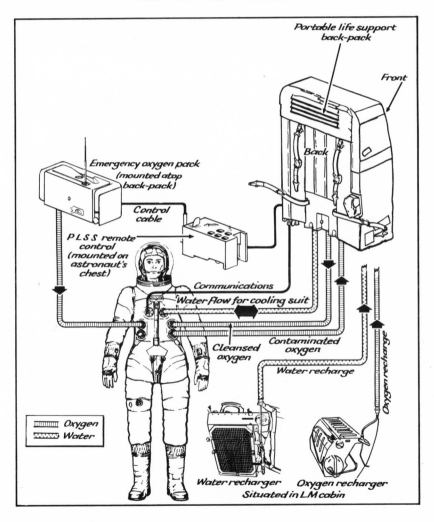

surface. He found that he could move about easily in his bulky white spacesuit and heavy backpack while under the influence of lunar gravity, which makes everything weigh only one-sixth of what it weighs on earth.

After 19 minutes, Armstrong was joined outside the landing craft by Aldrin, who had been preparing and handing down equipment for the two hours of probing and experimenting.

As Aldrin came through the hatch and started down the ladder, he said, "I want to back up and partially close the hatch, making sure not to lock it on my way out."

"Good thought," Armstrong agreed.

"That's our home for the next couple of hours," Aldrin added. "We want to take good care of it."

Then, as Aldrin started his first testing of the surface, Armstrong said: "Isn't this fun?"

"Right in this area I don't think there's much fine powder," Aldrin said. "It's hard to tell whether it's a clod or a rock."

"You can pick it up," Armstrong pointed out.

"And it bounces," was Aldrin's answer.

They immediately set up another TV camera away from the craft to give people on earth a broader look at the Sea of Tranquility landscape: a bleak, empty, almost flat, crater-pocked surface. Yet, Armstrong described the landscape as having "a stark beauty all its own."

"It's like much of the high desert of the United States," he said. "It's different but it's very pretty out here."

One of the first things the astronauts did was to plant their 3-by-5-foot American flag. It was stiffened with thin wire so as to appear to be flying on the windless lunar surface.

WALKING LIKE KANGAROOS

The astronauts found walking and working on the moon less

tiring than had been predicted. Armstrong once reported he was "very comfortable." Even with their heavy spacesuits and backpacks, the men bounded about easily in kangaroo, almost floating hops. "You do have to be rather careful to keep track of where your center of mass is," Aldrin observed after testing his agility. "Sometimes it takes about two or three paces to make sure that you've got your feet underneath you," he explained. "And about two to three, or maybe four, easy paces can bring you to a fairly smooth stop. Like a football player, you just have to put out to the side and cut a little bit. The so-called kangaroo hop—it does work, but it seems the forward ability is not quite as good as it is in the more conventional one foot after another. As far as saying what a safe pace might be—the one that I'm using now could get rather tiring after several hundred. But this may be a function of the suit as well as lack of gravity forces."

Aldrin discussed the problem of seeing into the dark shadows: "I've noticed several times in going from the sunlight into shadow that just as I go in I catch an additional reflection off the LEM that, along with reflection of my face into the visor, makes visibility very poor just as the transition of sunlight into shadow. Since we have so much glare coming onto my visor—shadow— and then it takes a short while for my eyes to adapt to the lighting conditions. Inside the shadow area, visibility is, as we said before, not too great. But with both visors up we can certainly see what sort of footprints we have and the condition of the soil. Then after being out in the sunlight a while it takes . . . watch it, Neil. Neil, you're on a cable. Yeah, lift up your right foot. Right foot. It's still hooked on it. Wait a minute. Okay, you're clear now."

It was an eerie scene, like a throwback to Buck Rogers science fiction. The black-and-white TV pictures of the lunar module and the astronauts were so sharp and clear as to seem unreal, more like a toy and toy-like figures than human beings on the most daring and far-reaching expedition thus far undertaken.

At one point the astronauts were suddenly interrupted by a summons from Houston. Then President Nixon came on a telephone-radio hookup to congratulate Armstrong and Aldrin in what, he said, "certainly has to be the most historic telephone call ever made." The conversation was televised at both ends and shown on a split screen, with the President in his oval office at the White House, and the astronauts standing in front of their landing craft.

"Because of what you have done," the President said, "the heavens have become a part of man's world. And as you talk to us from the Sea of Tranquility, it requires us to redouble our efforts to bring peace and tranquility to earth. For one priceless moment in the whole history of man, all the people on this earth are truly one—one in their pride in what you have done and one in our prayers that you will return safely to earth."

Armstrong, the Apollo 11 commander, answered: "Thank you, Mr. President. It's a great honor and privilege for us to be here representing not only the United States but men of peace of all nations, men with interests and a curiosity and men with a vision for the future."

The astronauts wasted no time settling down to their chores. Each had a checklist printed on one sleeve of his moonsuit. Aside from sending back TV pictures and descriptions of the moon, they had two objectives: (1) to set out three scientific experiments; (2) to collect up to 60 pounds of lunar rocks and soil.

For the first experiment, Armstrong and Aldrin set up a sheet of aluminum foil a foot wide and a yard long for a solar-wind test. Its purpose was to trap rare outflowing gases from the sun— such as argon, krypton, xenon, neon, and helium. The aluminum foil with captured gases was placed in a vacuum box to be returned to earth for study. Scientists hoped this "wind" would throw light on the way in which the sun and planets were formed.

The second experiment was an instrument to report any

tremors caused by falling meteorites or volcanic eruptions. The reports, it was hoped, would provide clues to the makeup of the moon.

The third experiment, also left on the moon, was a 2-foot-square laser reflector made up of 100 fused-silica prisms. Pointed toward the earth, it was designed to reflect a beam of light directly back to the earth. By measuring the travel time of the pulses to the moon and back, scientists could use the reflector to trace very small changes in earth-moon distances. These changes might show whether gravity was weakening or the continents shifting, and might provide sensitive tests of scientific theories.

MINING THE MOON

Of all the experimental tasks, however, top priority went to the collection of rocks and soil. The samples taken by Armstrong and Aldrin, both amateur geologists with special training, were headed for the Lunar Receiving Laboratory in Houston for initial tests, and then, after a period of quarantine, to other laboratories across the country for more thorough study.

Armstrong scooped up the first "contingency" sample and put it in his pant-leg pocket almost as soon as he got out of the lunar module. This was even before Aldrin descended, and was done to assure having some lunar material if something suddenly went wrong on the surface and the astronauts had to "abort" the mission.

"Like it's a little difficult to dig through the crust," Armstrong said as he gathered up the sample. "It's very interesting. It's a very soft surface but here and there where I plug with the contingency sample collector, I run into very hard surface, but it appears to be very cohesive material of the same sort."

Later, while Aldrin was busy with other tasks, Armstrong

went farther from the module and collected more rocks and soil at random. Aldrin then took his turn, making more careful choices within a radius of up to 100 feet of the craft, while Armstrong took pictures. Since the spacesuits did not allow the astronauts to bend more than slightly, the men used scoops and tongs with long handles. This first lunar geological prospecting was seen very clearly on home TV screens. As the astronauts walked about, they described by radio what they saw. They put the samples in sealed aluminum boxes for the trip back to earth.

Here is how some of the conversation went:

Armstrong: Now this one's right down front. And I want to know if you can see an angular rock in the foreground.

Houston: Roger, we have a large angular rock in the foreground. And it looks like a much smaller rock a couple of inches to the left.

Armstrong: And beyond it about 10 feet is an even larger rock that's rounded. That rock is about—the closest one to you is about—that one sticking out of the sand—about one foot. It's about a foot and a half long and it's about six inches thick. But it's standing on edge.

Aldrin: Neil, I've got the table out . . . and the bag deployed.

Houston: Roger. And we see the shadow of the LEM.

Armstrong: The little hill just beyond the shadow of the LEM is a pair of elongated craters, so they appear together as 40 feet long and 20 feet across and they're probably six feet deep. We'll probably get more work in there later.

Houston: Roger. And we see Buzz going about his work.

Armstrong reported that he collected about 50 pounds of soil and rock samples from several areas within the limited excursion sector around the lunar module. Most of the samples he scooped off the surface, but he went as deep as three inches. There was no noticeable change in the soil at that depth. He did not hit any hard bed. Armstrong said there was a wide variety of rocks, and the boulders were generally about two feet high.

The rocks were coated with surface powder, making them slippery in the deep vacuum that exists on the lunar surface. Some of the rocks were full of cavities. Another rock was said to look like a biotite, a dark green or black form of mica that is found on rocks on earth.

As one of their last acts on the lunar surface, the moon men drove coring tubes into the surface with a hammer to capture deeper material that would be sure not to show any changes from the heat of the lunar module's landing rocket blast. Aldrin said he had no trouble going in about 2 or 3 inches, but then had to pound "about as hard as I could." He drove the tube about 8 or 9 inches into the surface, then he noticed something puzzling.

For some reason, he said, the tube "didn't seem to want to stand upright. I'd keep driving it in and it would dig some sort of a hole, but it wouldn't penetrate in a way that it would support itself." He added that the material in the tube was "quite well packed, a good bit darker and the way it adhered to the core tube gave me the distinct impression of being moist."

All in all, man's first walk on the moon lasted 2 hours and Armstrong and Aldrin climbed back up into the Eagle where they continued to radio their impressions to Houston before resting.

Armstrong and Aldrin still had the risky lift-off to rejoin the orbiting Columbia command ship which Colonel Collins had been piloting all this time. The two astronauts were completely dependent upon the 3,500-pound-thrust ascent rocket in the upper half of the lunar module. If it failed to fire, they would be stranded.

CHAPTER 13

Home to Earth

Suspense on a space mission is always greatest when the ship is out of ground contact or is trying a maneuver for the first time. The suspense was never greater than on Monday, July 21, when Armstrong and Aldrin prepared to lift off the moon for the return home.

The ascent rocket in the upper half of the Lunar Module had been tested hundreds of times, of course; but never on the moon. And instead of a fully equipped launching pad for the lift-off, the astronauts had to trust the lunar module's lower half, which had been separated from the ascent stage by the firing of explosive bolts. At this point, the mission and the men's lives depended on these two pieces of equipment working perfectly.

But the engine fired on time and at full thrust. It lifted the ascent vehicle and sent it into a long orbital path toward a rendezvous with the waiting command ship. A sigh of relief went up at Mission Control in Houston as the lunar module radio reported: "Nine, eight, seven, six, five, first stage engine on ascent. Proceed. Beautiful. 26, 36 feet per second up. Little pitch over, very smooth, very quiet ride."

Four minutes later, the Eagle reported: "Eagle is back in orbit, having left Tranquility Base, and leaving behind a replica from our Apollo 11 patch with an olive branch."

That's not all the moon explorers left behind. On the site of the landing was the descent stage, no longer needed and therefore excess baggage. Around it, like the clutter left by some campers, were the cameras, walking boots, equipment boxes, an aluminum pole, two back packs and other equipment which the astronauts pitched out to lighten their load for take-off.

The lift-off came as Colonel Collins was piloting the command ship through its 25th revolution of the moon. Collins, who was somewhat of a forgotten man during the time his crewmates were performing their feats on the lunar surface, received an unofficial tribute from the space agency for doing the tasks usually shared by all three crewmen. The announcer at Mission Control said: "Not since Adam has any human known such solitude as Mike Collins is experiencing during the 47 minutes of each lunar revolution when he's behind the moon with no one to talk to except his tape recorder aboard Columbia."

Armstrong and Aldrin closed in for the rendezvous in a series of four maneuvers with the lunar module's smaller thruster jets. At about 69 miles above the front face of the moon, the Columbia joined its nose with the top hatch of the Eagle. As the two vehicles moved in for the link-up, their aim was off slightly; but the docking, though bumpy, was done without trouble.

Armstrong and Aldrin crawled through the connecting tunnel

to rejoin Collins, and then they jettisoned the lunar module, which became a piece of junk orbiting the moon. Finally, they fired the Apollo's main engine, boosting the craft out of lunar orbit for the 60-hour coasting voyage toward the splashdown in the Pacific.

ROUTINE TRIP BACK

The trip back was routine. Until the last few hours before splashdown, the astronauts had little work to do except for checking spacecraft systems, performing housekeeping chores, and conducting more television shows for the folks at home.

On one telecast Aldrin showed how easy it was to apply ham spread to a slice of bread, which he grabbed out of mid-air in the cabin. Collins took a playful drink by holding the water gun a few inches from his mouth and squirting the water in, much as a Spaniard drinking from a wineskin. Armstrong said: "No matter where you travel, it is nice to get home."

On another telecast the astronauts talked about what they had been through. Collins said, "This trip of ours to the moon may have looked simple and easy. I want to assure you that this has not been the case." He pointed out all the complex equipment involved, and talked about the thousands of workers "below the surface" who made the mission possible.

"We've come to the conclusion," Aldrin added, "that this has been far more than three men on a voyage to the moon, more still than the efforts of a government and industry team, more even than the efforts of one nation. We feel that this stands as a symbol of the insatiable curiosity of all mankind to explore the unknown."

It was on their trip back that the astronauts learned that the Soviet Union's unmanned spacecraft, Luna 15, which had held the world in suspense for more than a week, had apparently crashed into the moon's surface. Launched three days ahead of Apollo 11, Luna 15 was regarded by many observers as a Soviet rival to the American spacecraft. The Russians announced Tuesday morning that Luna 15 had "reached the moon's surface" and that its work had "ended." The fact that it went out of action as soon as it touched the lunar surface suggested that it was not a soft landing but a crash.

At 12:22 P.M. Thursday, the astronauts jettisoned the service module, the equipment section carrying the rocket engine, to start the final descent from 400,000 feet into the earth's atmosphere. When they reached the atmosphere, the earth's gravity was exerting such a pulling force that the capsule was traveling at more than 24,000 miles an hour. Then the earth's air gripped at the spacecraft, slowing its speed.

SAFELY HOME

Within minutes, the astronauts were in the water 950 miles southwest of Hawaii—home safe from man's first trip to the moon. The splashdown was one minute earlier than the time scheduled in the original flight plan. Waiting to welcome them aboard the recovery aircraft carrier, the U.S.S. Hornet, 11 miles away, was President Nixon. He was in the Pacific area en route to a tour of Asian countries.

"All three of us are excellent," the Apollo men radioed from their bobbing capsule. "Take your time."

The astronauts were given biological isolation garments by a frogman as soon as the hatch was open, as part of the quarantine program designed to avoid moon germs. And they were washed off when they climbed into a raft to await the recovery helicopter.

President Nixon watched the recovery proceedings from the Hornet's bridge, but he had to wait 55 minutes to talk with them after they reached the deck of the carrier. The helicopter that brought them was immediately towed to an elevator for lowering to the flight deck where the astronauts went into the mobile isolation trailer for a quick checkup.

When the meeting finally came, the smiling astronauts were peeking out a window of the van. Now wearing blue coveralls, the men appeared relaxed and happy as they jostled each other to look out the window. The President, with the band playing "Hail to the Chief," strode briskly down the carpet to the front of the van. He stood about three feet from the astronauts and spoke to them through a microphone-speaker hookup:

"Neil, Buzz, and Mike, I want you to know that I think I'm the luckiest man in the world, and I say this not only because I have the honor to be President of the United States, but particularly because I have the privilege of speaking for so many in welcoming you back to earth.

"I can tell you about all the messages we have received in Washington, over 100 foreign governments, emperors and presidents and prime ministers and kings, have sent the most warm messages that we've ever received.

"They represent over two billion people on this earth, all of them who have had the opportunity to see what you have done."

As throngs of sailors listened on the deck and millions of people watched on home television screens, Mr. Nixon then chatted with the astronauts about baseball, world news, the splashdown, and phone calls he made to their wives, "three of the greatest ladies," inviting them and the astronauts to a state dinner. In the middle of the banter, he suddenly blurted, "Gee, you look great! You feel as good as you look?"

"I feel just perfect, Mr. President," Armstrong, the Apollo commander, replied.

Then the President grew serious again:

"I was thinking as you know as you came down and we knew

it was a success and it had only been eight days—just a week, a long week—but this is the greatest week in the history of the world since the Creation. Because of what happened in this week, the world is bigger infinitely and also as I'm going to find in this trip around the world, and Secretary [of State William] Rogers will find as he covers the other countries in Asia, as a result of what you've done, the world's never been closer together before.

"And we just thank you for that, and I only hope that all of us in government, all of us in America, that as a result of what you've done we could do our job a little better, we can reach for the stars just as you have reached so far for the stars."

Armstrong, again answering for the crew, said: "We're just pleased to be back and very honored that you were so kind as to come out here and welcome us back, and we look forward to getting out of this quarantine and talking."

At the end of the short ceremony, the President waved to them and walked back to return to the deck. As he left, the astronauts waved out the window at the cheering sailors. Then they, too, turned into their isolation van to continue their quarantine.

The astronauts were scheduled to spend three days in the mobile trailer while it was shipped by the Hornet to Hawaii, thence by plane and truck to the Lunar Receiving Laboratory in Houston. There they were to remain in quarantine until August 11, going through post-flight debriefings. The 50 pounds of lunar rocks and soil they brought back were shipped immediately to the lab for study.

The completion of the great mission triggered celebrations across the nation, particularly at the control centers and at the homes of the astronauts' families. At Mission Control in Houston, the men stood up at their consoles, cheered, waved small American flags, and talked of flying men to Mars. On a small screen there appeared the Eagle emblem of the Apollo 11 and the words: "Task Accomplished. July 1969."

CHAPTER 14

Moon
Treasure

Even before the three astronauts left their recovery ship, a small but precious cargo, the treasure of Apollo 11, was rushed to the Manned Spacecraft Center in Houston. The treasure was the rocks and soil Armstrong and Aldrin had scooped up from the moon's surface at Tranquility Base. The astronauts had packed and sealed the samples, which weighed about 48 pounds, in two air-tight aluminum containers each about the size of a small suitcase. The "rock boxes," as they were called, were transported separately from the ship to Ellington Air Force Base so that the whole shipment could not be lost in a single accident. About 24 hours after splashdown, the first box arrived at Ellington, where it was welcomed after the fashion of returning astronauts. Thomas O.

Paine, the NASA administrator, had personally escorted the box from the Hornet, and most of the high-level officials of the space center were standing on the tarmac as the giant jet cargo plane taxied to a stop. They saw to it that the box was safely transferred to a white panel truck with glass sides and then transported the five miles from Ellington to the Lunar Receiving Laboratory (LRL) for the beginning of months of painstaking scientific analysis.

Awaiting the moon samples were the 26 scientists who made up the preliminary examination team. They could hardly contain their jittery eagerness. "Scientifically, this will be worth more than any other material in history," said Elbert W. King, curator of the LRL.

On Saturday afternoon, July 26, scientists got their first look at the moon rocks. Four selected geologists—Clifford Frondel of Harvard University, Edward Chao of the United States Geological Survey, Robin Brett of the Manned Spacecraft Center, and King— watched the opening of the first box through a porthole in a vacuum chamber where conditions closely approximated those on the air-less moon. Jack Warren, an LRL technician, worked from outside the chamber. In this way, he was able to manipulate the box without contaminating it. While looking through a porthole, Warren inserted a needle through the box's wall to draw off and collect any gases that might have been given off by the rocks. Then he unlatched the lid, removed the upper layer of packing material, and lifted out a piece of aluminum foil that had been used to trap solar particles and the two lunar core samples. Finally, Warren removed the plastic-wrapped rocks with his gloved hands and cut open the top. "This moment," Brett said in his Australian accent, "is the beginning of the study of lunar rocks on earth. To earth scientists this is a very, very exciting time."

It was a tantalizing and frustrating experience, for the scientists found a coating of blackish, fine-grained dust made it impossible for them to determine immediately the nature or true color of the moon rocks. All Frondel could say was, "We have a box full of rocks coated by this layer of black material." Describing the way the dust seemed to stick to the rocks, Frondel said that he would like to "give them the good scrubbing they deserve."

In the days that followed, the laboratory technicians and geologists brushed the dust off the rocks and began to see what they had. The first box contained 20 rocks, weighing a total of about 17 pounds. The largest rock in the sample was estimated to be about seven inches long, five inches wide and two inches thick. The second box was opened August 4. It contained 31 pounds of fine-grained soil and rocks. Some rocks were as large as cobblestones and others as small as golf balls.

About two weeks after the rocks arrived in the LRL, I was among a dozen newsmen who gathered in the viewing room at the laboratory for the public's first look at one of the moon rocks. One expected, almost demanded, that the rock be spectacularly different. But there it was, in lonely splendor behind the plate glass window, a small, gray rock flecked with tiny crystals and bearing a faint tint of pinkish brown. The rock, about three inches long and $1\frac{1}{4}$ inches thick, was enclosed in a glass vacuum jar. It seemed very ordinary.

Upon closer examination, the rock did have some distinctive characteristics, primarily the tiny pits. Most of the pits were seen under a microscope to have black, glassy bottoms with white halos. This indicated, the geologists said, that long after the rock was formed it was bombarded by high-velocity particles, probably micrometeorites or fragments sent flying by impacts elsewhere on the moon. The white rings suggested that the heat generated by the impacts produced additional crystallization.

While it contained no hitherto unknown elements, the rock seemed to have the familiar elements in different proportions and different arrangements than earth rocks. As one scientist put it, "It's the same alphabet but a different grammar."

RUSH TO JUDGMENT

Such was the moon's complexity that many of the scientists' earliest conclusions, announced rather breathlessly in the first weeks, turned out to be misleading. For example, scientists who briefed newsmen at the Houston space center were on the verge of discarding the cold-moon theory. The geologists announced that the rocks were igneous, which meant that they had solidified from molten material. Finding igneous rocks, instead of sedimentary rocks, seemed to eliminate the interesting but far-out hypothesis that the moon's *maria*, or plains, were sedimentary deposits from former bodies of water. Instead, the rocks must have been melted at some time in the moon's past, either by heat generated in a collision with a large meteorite or through a volcanic eruption. When the geologists confirmed the presence of vesicles in some of the rocks, the weight of evidence seemed to be tipped in favor of the "hot-mooners." Vesicles are the tiny holes formed as gases escape, a promising sign of volcanic activity in connection with the rocks' formation. One after another, geologists mentioned what they said was evidence of past volcanic activity. The hot-moon bandwagon was rolling, and shortly Eugene A. Shoemaker, one of the chief investigators, proclaimed that the composition of some of the rocks agreed broadly with volcanic rocks on earth. The evidence of a hot moon, Shoemaker concluded, was "overwhelming."

At that point, Harold C. Urey, the 76-year-old Nobel Prize-winning chemist from the University of California at San Diego and a long-time advocate of the cold, dead moon theory, rose from his seat near the front of the space center auditorium. He seemed stunned and perplexed. His white head was shaking as he acknowledged that the lunar samples "look as though they could be lava flows." Said Urey: "I have thought for twenty years that we had a cold moon. I would say that on the basis of the present evidence . . . I shall certainly consider very carefully whether I should not revise that opinion."

Many of the bright young geologists who were hot-mooners jubilantly claimed victory. Of Urey, some said that he was a great scientist "but is, well, a little on." Their victory was fleeting, however. A few days later, as a result of elaborate chemical dating methods, it became clear that the Apollo 11 rocks were about 3.6 billion years old—not, as the hot-mooners had assumed, a relatively young 100 or so million years old. Thus, the moon may have been hot once, but that was long, long ago. In that case, the moon, as Urey had long predicted, might well be a relic of the solar system's earliest history and, therefore, be of even greater interest to scientists. Urey's opponents backed down. "You know that Harold is the grandfather of lunar science," they were saying with restored modesty. "Don't let anyone tell you he isn't as sharp as he ever was."

The lunar scientists had learned a lesson: There were no quick answers. The moon, they now realized, would yield its secrets grudgingly.

DOWN TO WORK

After the initial confusion and controversy, the scientists settled down to one of the most intensive studies in the history of science. The samples from Apollo 11—and later from Apollos 12 and 14—were X-rayed and photographed through powerful electron microscopes. They were dipped in chemicals and picked apart grain by tiny grain. They were ground up and fed to bacteria, plants and laboratory animals. They were probed for radioactive decay as a measure of their age.

The first definitive reports on their studies were made in January 1970 at the Lunar Science Conference in Houston. A second conference was held a year later after scientists had had more time to consider what they had learned. At those conferences, the scientists still did not always agree with each other. They argued in the formal sessions, in the corridors, and late into the night. But by the end of the second conference, the scientists had sorted through their data and reached some general conclusions about the moon.

ANY LIFE, ANY WATER?

One question was answered early and fairly conclusively. Was there life on the moon? Had there ever been any? Safety of the people working with the samples, as well as curiosity, demanded a quick answer through a search for the presence of any kind of microorganisms.

Bits of lunar dust were placed under the skins of laboratory mice and in oysters and other life forms to test for any organic substances, especially for any toxic activity. None was found. Other scientists placed lunar dust and rock chips under a 300,-000-power microscope and could see no sign of lunar organisms, living, dead or fossilized. Moreover, results indicated that the amounts of organic compounds, which are associated with living organisms on earth, were negligible in the lunar samples—less than 200 parts per billion. It was hard to tell whether these compounds originated on the moon or were mere earthly contaminants. But scientists concluded that there was no life on the moon.

Neither could they find any trace of water. At the 1971 Lunar Science Conference, David R. Wones of the Massachusetts

Institute of Technology concluded that "the moon is very dry and always has been exceedingly dry." He said: "There's no evidence for any water at all from the moon itself. And most of the hydrogen that's been reported [in the samples] appear to be from the solar wind or from contaminants."

TWO KINDS OF ROCKS

The rock samples returned by Apollo astronauts fell into two broad categories—igneous and breccia.

The igneous rocks crystallized from molten material that had to be at least 2,100 degrees Fahrenheit. According to some scientists, the molten material may have extended as deep as 100 to 200 miles. But the rocks did not reveal whether the moon got so hot through internal (volcanic) or external (meteorite) forces, or a combination of both.

Most of the Apollo 11 and 12 igneous rocks were a dark gray color. They contained various proportions of four minerals common on earth: pyroxene, plagioclase feldspar, olivine and ilmenite. George H. Morrison and his colleagues at Cornell University detected traces of 68 chemical elements in the Apollo 11 rocks. The concentrations of titanium, zirconium, lithium and barium ran from three to 10 times higher than in earth rocks. Pure iron was in greater abundance, as was chromium. "It would be very difficult to make an earth rock with these components," said Ross Taylor, a New Zealand geochemist on the preliminary examination team for Apollo 11, referring to the strange chemical proportions.

The rocks called breccias were conglomerates of fragments of igneous rock compacted with lunar soil. In Apollo 11, half the samples were breccias; in Apollo 12, only 20 per cent were breccias. Lunar breccias were presumably formed as a result of impacts of meteorites. The pressures on impact could be so great, scientists concluded, as to weld the mixture of soil and rock fragments into solid rock.

To determine the ages of both the igneous and breccia rocks, scientists analyzed, by the rubidium-strontium dating method, the decay rate of radioactive elements in the samples. Through such analysis, the scientists discovered that the Apollo 11 rocks crystallized about 3.6 to 3.7 billion years ago. Nearly all of the Apollo 12 rocks were found to be somewhat younger, about 3.3 to 3.4 billion years old. This finding destroyed some of the hot-moon theories and encouraged scientists in their belief that the ancient moon contained clues to the solar system's early history.

A BLANKET OF DUST AND BEADS

Besides the rocks, the lunar samples consisted of tiny soil fragments. Some were as fine as powdery dust. Some were tiny spheres of glass, one of the most distinctive features discovered by Apollo. This dust and glass, the product of millions and millions of years of meteorite bombardment, made up the topsoil at all the early Apollo landing sites. At Tranquility Base, the topsoil—regolith, the geologists call it—was estimated to be between 9 and 18 feet thick, averaging about 12 feet and becoming more compact at the greater depths. If the bedrock at Tranquility was an estimated 3.7 billion years old and the regolith's thickness was an average 12 feet, then it was estimated that the average rate of regolith formation on the moon is on the order of one millimeter per million years. By earth standards, this is extremely slow.

The glass beads, which were found at all the Apollo sites, ranged from microscopic size to the size of a sand granule. They were multicolored, from dark brown and amber to yellow and clear. Some of the stereoscopic color pictures taken by Armstrong showed glassy splashes fused onto the tops of small rocks. "The surprise is not in their existence," Harvard's Clifford Frondel said of the glass spheres, "but in their abundance." Frondell suggested that the glass was formed when a meteorite smashed into the surface and generated such heat as to vaporize silica-rich lunar material. The glass probably condensed out of the vapor, solidified and rained on the moon.

By burning a batch of lunar soil and studying the different colors of its elements in the flame, it was possible to determine that the soil contained more than 70 elements. Another test of the soil indicated that the moon promised to be an excellent place to study the composition of the sun. When he heated a pinch of lunar dust to 3,000 degrees Fahrenheit, Oliver A. Schaeffer of the State University of New York at Stony Brook discovered in the escaping gases a surprisingly rich lode of the atomic particles that boil off the sun as the so-called solar wind. Schaeffer found a large amount of helium, argon, neon, krypton and xenon. "We expected to find traces," Schaeffer said, "but we found bucketsful of solar wind."

But the most surprising and puzzling of discoveries about the lunar soil concerned its age. By every dating method, the soil was found to be 4.4 to 4.6 billion years old—as old as the moon itself and almost a billion years older than most of the surrounding rocks.

ROCK 13 AND THE AGE PARADOX

Why was the lunar soil so much older than the rocks? If the soil had obviously formed from the pulverization of the rocks, how could the soil be older than the rocks? When scientists tried unsuccessfully to make chemical models of the rocks out of the elements found in the soil, they began to suspect the answer to the puzzle. The soil apparently contained material from the original moon that was no longer in the rocks. The strange elements in the lunar soil were called "the magic component," or "the cryptic factor." Paul W. Gast, chief of earth and planetary sciences at the Manned Spacecraft Center, defined the material with the word "kreep," an acronym for the chemical symbols of potassium (K), rare earth elements (REE) and phosphorous (P). These radioactive elements were found in greater abundance in the lunar soil than in the rocks.

Then, among the Apollo 12 samples, scientists found a single walnut-sized rock that set off a new wave of excitement. When the rock's radioactivity was tested at the LRL in Houston, the results were startling. The rock contained ten times as much potassium, thorium and uranium as the Apollo 11 rocks and as much as 40 times the concentrations in other Apollo 12 rocks. The rock seemed to be a sample of what the scientists were seeking—the magic component or kreep.

The rock was labeled 12013. The 12 stood for Apollo 12 and the 13 represented the order in which the rock had been drawn from the sample box. But scientists came to call it simply Rock 13. From it two thin slices were cut with a diamond-studded saw, and only these were let out of the laboratory for analysis.

The next surprise about Rock 13 was its age. In May 1970, I was visiting Gerald Wasserburg of Caltech at his laboratory on the campus in Pasadena. A brass plate over the door read: Lunatic Asylum. His colleagues playfully called themselves inmates, and the machine that was developed for highly accurate radioactive dating of samples was called Lunatic 1. "We got the famous Rock 13 in there," Wasserburg said as he rushed out from his laboratory, hitching his Indian belt and straightening his bolo tie. "It's a real weirdo."

Only a few minutes earlier Wasserburg had discovered that Rock 13—or at least part of it—was about 4.5 billion years old.

It was as old as the lunar soil with all its magic components. It was almost as old as the moon. Could Rock 13 then have been part of the crust formed from a once-molten moon?

As more data came out of a computer, Wasserburg said: "This rock stands in a unique position, if these numbers are correct. All of the other lunar samples returned have lost their memory of the earliest processes in the solar system. This is the first candidate brought from the moon to give us this view of early processes."

The ages of the rocks—Rock 13 and the younger samples from Tranquility Base and the Ocean of Storms—gave scientists some important clues to the moon's early history. Rock 13 was the first firm evidence that somewhere on the moon there is a relatively undisturbed record of the processes that shaped the earth and other planets. The difference of about 300 million years between the time of crystallization of the standard Apollo 11 and Apollo 12 rocks indicated that those two large "seas" were the result of two distinct melting processes. And those events were presumably distinct from the earlier processes that formed Rock 13 and the highlands from which it apparently came. Finally, the ages indicated that, though it appears cold and dead now, the moon, or parts of it, was hot at least as recently as 3.3 billion years ago. It was now clear that the moon was more complex than either the hot-mooners or the cold-mooners had ever imagined.

EROSION, TRACKS AND TREMORS

The moon has not gone completely unchanged since the cataclysmic events that shaped its crust and great plains. Cratering has been the most obvious process for change over the millions of years. But scientists, examining the Apollo rocks and surface photographs, also discovered that the lunar topsoil was subject to a slow but definite turnover. Moreover, there was some kind of erosion occurring on the moon.

The churning of the lunar surface came about largely from the cratering process. Impacts from meteorites, large and microscopic, dredged up rocks and soil from depths of several feet, buried surface rocks and sent other rocks tossing, turning and rolling.

Microscopic tracks in lunar rocks and soil provided additional evidence of surface churning and a fairly good estimate of how long any particular rock had been on the surface. These tracks were etched by the bombardment of particles from the solar wind and cosmic rays.

The best estimates of exposure ages came from the cosmic-ray tracts. Cosmic rays are high-energy particles generated by unknown sources in outer space. They travel with such high momentum that they can cause the splitting of atoms with which they collide. If one of the products of such fission is radioactive, then the ratio of the fission product to the parent element can be ascertained and the time of the collision estimated. In this way, scientists measured cosmic-ray exposure times ranging from less than one million years on the surface to as much as 450 million years. A single boulder on earth seldom survives atmospheric weathering for more than a few thousand years.

Another source of continuing natural disturbance on the moon is the occasional moonquake. The Apollo 11 seismometer, dependent on solar energy for power, operated for only a few weeks. But the Apollo 12 seismometer, running on nuclear energy, transmitted a wealth of data for more than a year. There were many surprises in the data.

When the upper stage of the Apollo 12 Lunar Module was sent crashing into the moon, the impact was detected by the Apollo 12 seismometer. The impact sent off seismic waves lasting more than 50 minutes; on earth a similar impact should have caused no more than a few minutes of vibration. The duration and pattern of the seismic wave led scientists to speculate that the Ocean of Storms was underlain with rock rubble to great depths before any solid layer was encountered. This would account for resonating vibrations like sound waves inside a bell. Later impacts produced even longer seismic signals, some of which cannot be adequately explained on the basis of present knowledge of the moon's interior.

The seismometer also detected 208 tremors, caused either by meteorite impact or by moonquakes, during an eight-month period. Nearly all of them occurred each month when the moon came closest to the earth. Scientists naturally inferred that the increased tug of earth gravity produced tidal stresses on the moon, causing some shifting and shaking of its outer shell. The moonquakes occurred frequently along the lunar rills, narrow or deep canyons which may be "fault zones" where slight movements in the surface are taking place.

It was thought that the moonquakes alone did not justify any conclusion that the moon had a hot interior like the earthquake-prone earth. The moonquakes seldom reached depths of more than half a mile. If that is generally true of the moon, Apollo scientists concluded, the low level of seismic activity could mean that the moon's outer shell is far more rigid and stable than earth's.

THE STILL MYSTERIOUS MOON

Some questions had been settled, but the basic ones still perplexed scientists after the early Apollo landings. There appeared to be no water or life on the moon, now or ever before. The dust on the surface was pervasive, but not the hazard it was once thought to be when some scientists feared the astronauts might be buried in it. There were no new, strange chemical elements on the moon, only strange, unexplained ways the chemicals sometimes were concentrated in certain rocks. There was an abundance of beautiful glassy spheres on the moon, of gases from the sun and of cosmicray tracks from particles originating in unknown places in outer space. There were rocks as old as the solar system, presumably the "Rosetta Stone" scientists had hoped to find on the moon.

What could not be settled immediately and conclusively was the most controversial question of all: How did the moon come to be? Three theories of lunar origin had been debated for years before Apollo 11. The first theory held that the moon was torn from the earth by a fission process. The second was that the moon was formed at the same time as the earth as a sort of twin planet. The third theory was that the moon was unrelated to earth and was captured by earth's gravity at some time in the past.

Weighing what had been learned by Apollo, Robin Brett, one of NASA's chief geologists, concluded: "All three theories have weaknesses in the light of our present knowledge. The composition of the returned lunar samples makes it difficult to derive them from anything like the composition of the earth's mantle. This, therefore, makes the fission theory extremely unlikely. And if the moon was formed as an identical twin planet with the same composition as the earth's mantle, the same argument applies against that theory. The capture theory presents difficulties in celestial mechanics and is regarded as statistically fairly improbable. It seems much easier to explain the non-existence of the moon than its existence."

It was, indeed, one of the toughest jobs ever undertaken by scientists. There were many clues but few supportable theories. The scientists generally agreed that the moon was partly melted in its early history, underwent cataclysmic changes at the time the seas were created and is to some extent a layered body. They also agreed with Columbia University's Gary Latham that theirs was "the most exciting business in the world."

CHAPTER 15

Return to the Moon

If the moon could be visited once, it could be visited again and again, and so it was.

APOLLO 12: AT THE OCEAN OF STORMS

On November 19, 1970, when Apollo 12 Commander Charles "Pete" Conrad stepped down the ladder onto the surface of the moon, his mind raced back to the historic remark made by his predecessor. His eyes measured the long step from the bottom rung down to the moon. "Whoopie, man," Conrad, who was only 5 feet 6 inches tall, radioed to Mission Control, "that may have been a small step for Neil, but that's a long one for me."

With that light-hearted beginning, Pete Conrad and his co-pilot Alan L. Bean set out to demonstrate the many accomplishments that are possible by men who reach the moon. "The name of the game in Apollo 12 is lunar surface exploration," Conrad said before the flight. "Let's face it. Anything we got scientifically off Apollo 11 was a bonus."

Apollo 12's general target was a rolling plain known as the Ocean of Storms. The specific landing point lay just below the equator about 950 miles west of Armstrong and Aldrin's Tranquility Base.

But first, Conrad, Bean and the third crew member, Richard F. Gordon Jr., had to get to the moon—a prospect that looked bleak for a few moments on launching day, November 14. The hardware for Apollo 12 was essentially the same as for Apollo 11, and the countdown had gone smoothly. The only problem was the dark clouds that gathered over Cape Kennedy on launch morning. Since no manned spacecraft had ever been launched in the rain, it appeared that President Nixon, who was there for his first Apollo launching, would be disappointed. But the countdown continued when surveillance planes reported no electricity in the clouds. On schedule, at 11:22 A.M., the Saturn 5's five engines ignited and Apollo 12 roared slowly off the launching pad and up into the low-hanging clouds. Two bolts of lightning flashed out of the dark clouds, and simultaneously there was a sudden shutdown of the spacecraft's electrical system. Warning lights flashed on all over the cockpit control panels. Key components in the spacecraft's guidance system were knocked out, but a battery-powered secondary system took over until the astronauts could reset their circuit breakers.

"I don't know what happened," Conrad said. "We had everything in the world drop out. I think she must have been hit by lightning."

Though it was only a guess on his part, it turned out to be correct. But despite a momentary blackout, all seemed to be in good shape and the flight continued without incident. A NASA board of inquiry later decided that lightning had indeed caused the electrical crisis, but the lightning was generated by the rocket, not by the clouds.

On November 17, Apollo 12 fired its Service Module rocket to swing into lunar orbit. Two days later, Conrad and Bean rode their Lunar Module, *Intrepid*, down to the Ocean of Storms. To most men the wild ride of the LM, with its descent engine thundering and its attitude control jets slewing it from side to side, would have been a sobering experience. But those listening anxiously from earth heard joyous exclamations from Apollo 12.

"Pete, there it is! There it is! Son of a gun!" Bean shouted to Conrad. "Right down the middle of the road! Outstanding!"

"Hey," Conrad interrupted, "we're started right for the center of a crater. Look out there! I can't believe it. Amazing! Fantastic! Forty-two degrees, babe. Just keep talking."

Conrad kept his eye on the crater until *Intrepid's* engine kicked up so much lunar dust that the astronauts had to fly blind for the last 30 seconds. They were enveloped in a cloud of dust. Then contact.

High overhead, Gordon radioed from the command ship, *Yankee Clipper*, "I have *Intrepid*. I have *Intrepid*. . . . He is on the Surveyor crater about a fourth of a Surveyor crater diameter to the northwest."

Apollo 12 had made its pinpoint landing and was ready for the work at hand.

During their 31½-hour visit on the moon, Conrad and Bean took two hikes of about four hours each. Conrad started the first excursion at 6:45 A.M. Eastern Standard Time on November 19. From the foot of the Lunar Module ladder, Conrad looked around at the nearest crater and exclaimed, "Boy, you'll never believe it! Guess what I see sitting on the side of the crater. The old Surveyor!"

The "old Surveyor," 600 feet away, had been resting there

for two and a half years, its batteries and camera and communications dead but its structure practically unchanged in the airless environment. The Surveyor would be the astronauts' objective on their second hike. But first they had to set up some scientific instruments.*

The two men tramped about 1,000 feet from the landing craft to set up an array of instruments, the Apollo Lunar Surface Experiments Package, or ALSEP. The package, far more elaborate than Apollo 11's, included a passive seismometer, a magnetometer, a solar-wind spectrometer, a superthermal ion detector, and a cold cathode ion gauge. ALSEP's central station consisted of a small nuclear power plant to handle data processing from the various instruments and to receive radio commands from earth and to transmit a steady stream of data back to earth. With ALSEP instruments, scientists on earth could monitor a variety of phenomena: tremors from moonquakes and meteorite impacts, changes in local magnetism, the direction and intensity of the supersonic solar wind blowing out from the sun, and the presence of any traces of gas that might constitute a thin lunar atmosphere.

Their second four-hour excursion amounted to man's first "nature hike" on the moon. Conrad and Bean laughed and enjoyed themselves tremendously as they ranged far from their landing craft, stopping at small craters, taking core samples from beneath the surface dust, loping easily over the sometime dimpled and wrinkled lunar surface. Only once in a while did the astronauts' comments bring home the hazards. "Watch that crater behind you," Conrad called to Bean at one point. "Don't step back."

---

* Early in the first lunar walk, the astronauts accidentally pointed the lens of their television camera into the sun. The sunlight, being unscreened by any atmosphere, destroyed the camera's tube. People on earth were thus unable to see the rest of the first walk or any of the second walk by the Apollo 12 astronauts.

Despite the length of their walk, the astronauts reported they were feeling fine and not getting tired. "Do you know what I feel like, Al?" Conrad asked as they were taking those long, loping steps in the low gravity. "Did you ever see those pictures of giraffes running in slow motion? That's exactly what I feel like."

The lower gravity made for other strange effects. Conrad fell down once during the second lunar walk. But contrary to the fears of many Apollo planners, he had no trouble getting to his feet. He said that he got up by raising his body with a one-arm push-up and then pulling his feet under his body. Besides, Conrad explained, "You fall so slowly that you just start moving out again, keep moving until your feet come back under you."

Despite a few falls, the astronauts reached the forlorn Surveyor and found it "in very good shape." Using a pair of metal cutters, the astronauts removed the spacecraft's television camera, a painted aluminum strut, an electrical cable and its robot-like mechanical scoop, which had been used for the first digging into lunar soil. They had to work with extreme care. If they brushed against a ragged edge or any sharp object on the craft, the astronauts could tear their spacesuits, allowing their life-supporting oxygen to escape. But engineers back on earth were particularly eager to examine the parts to see what changes occur in materials that remain exposed to the lunar environment for two and a half years. This could help them design instruments for future spacecraft and for lunar bases.

Although most of the spacecraft was painted white when it left earth in April 1967, the astronauts found that it had turned tan. Surveyor engineers said that they knew that white paint, when exposed to ultraviolet radiation, would turn yellow. The tan color might have come from lunar dust as well as radiation.

From the Surveyor parts scientists discovered that it was possible for germs to live in the vacuum of space. Several months after the camera was brought back to Houston, a microbiologist succeeded in culturing a colony of bacteria from a small piece of polyurethane foam that had been inside the camera's circuitry. The bacteria were identical to a common form of microbes found in the human respiratory tract. It was, therefore, not an alien life form. And it was protected from the astronauts themselves. Consequently, scientists were left with the conclusion that the germs had survived nearly 1,000 days, protected in the camera, in an otherwise inhospitable environment.

On November 20, the Apollo 12 astronauts blasted off the moon, rejoined Gordon in the Command Ship and began their return trip to earth. Apollo 12, man's second voyage to a lunar landing, ended with a safe and smooth splashdown in the Pacific Ocean on November 24. Conrad, Bean and Gordon had made moon flight seem not only fun but almost routine. Or so it seemed until the flight of Apollo 13 five months later.

SOVIET STRATEGY

While the United States continued its moon drive, the Soviet Union pushed its space program in different directions. In October 1969, just before Apollo 12, Mstislav V. Keldysh, president of the Soviet Academy of Sciences, said that his country had no immediate plans to match the Apollo exploits. Instead, Keldysh said, "We are concentrating wholly on the creation of large satellite systems." To most American observers Keldysh's remarks confirmed what they had suspected for some time: The Soviet Union's primary thrust was the space station.

A space station will be a large vehicle with complex electronics, room for scientists as well as astronauts, an oxygen supply for many months of operations, attached laboratories and shuttlecraft for moving men and supplies to and from earth. Assembling such a cluster of vehicles, housing perhaps a dozen or more men, would involve sending up several spacecraft by several rockets and then maneuvering them to a rendezvous and link-up. The result would be the spaceship of the future.

When the Soviet Union launched three spacecraft, Soyuz 6, 7 and 8, in a week-long mission in October, it became clear that the earth-orbiting space station held a high priority in the Soviet scheme of things. But if the Russians had meant the mission as the beginning of the first actual space station, they fell short of their goal. There were no link-ups of vehicles, no transfers of crews between ships, and no test of the effects of long-duration weightlessness.

Nonetheless, the Russians did prove that they were able to launch three manned spacecraft in three consecutive days, which the United States had not done, and control their flights simultaneously. The Russians also demonstrated the first welding in space, a capability that would probably be essential in larger space stations.

In June 1970, the Russians launched another Soyuz—Soyuz 9. Two cosmonauts, Andrian G. Nikolayev and Vitaly I. Sevastyanov, were launched into earth orbit on June 1, and it soon became evident that Soyuz 9 was to be an endurance test. For almost 300 orbits, or more than 7 million miles, the two cosmonauts traveled around earth. The two men survived the flight in generally good health and on June 19 rode their Soyuz to a landing back in the Soviet Union. In all, they had orbited the earth for 17 days, 16 hours and 59 minutes—a new endurance record. The longest American flight was Gemini 7's 14 days in earth orbit. Although the cosmonauts experienced some difficulties acclimating themselves to life back in earth gravity, the mission was declared a success and "the beginning of long manned space flights" of the space-station era.

The Russians, however, had not lost sight of the moon. In

September 1970, Luna 16 landed on the moon's Sea of Fertility, about 200 miles east of Tranquility Base. It was a four-legged craft that vaguely resembled the LM descent stage. But soon the differences became apparent. On commands from ground controllers, Luna 16's mechanical arm reached out and began drilling 14 inches into the lunar surface. Then another robot arm extended and scooped up three ounces of soil and deposited it in a container in the upper capsule, which was later automatically sealed. Upon completion of the operation, the capsule rocketed off the moon, leaving the lower stage where it landed, and returned to earth. It was the first time a remote-controlled spacecraft had landed on the moon and returned to earth. In announcing the achievement, Soviet scientists hailed it as a much less expensive and safer way to explore the moon. An analysis of the samples showed that the Sea of Fertility soil was quite similar to the soil from the Sea of Tranquility and Ocean of Storms.

Two months later, the Russians unveiled another method of exploring the moon without men. Luna 17 landed on the Sea of Rains in November and released an eight-wheel, solar-powered vehicle for moving out from the landing site to take pictures and record scientific data. The vehicle, called Lunokhod 1, was a large pot-bellied tank with a top that opened like a clamshell, the upper half serving as a receptor of solar energy to run the machine. The Lunokhod was operated for several months in what appeared to be primarily engineering tests of such machinery.

The Soviet successes with Luna 16 and Luna 17 received all the more attention because the most recent American expedition to the moon, Apollo 13, had been a breathtaking failure.

APOLLO 13: "WE'VE GOT A PROBLEM"

The motto of Apollo 13 was the Latin phrase *Ex luna, scientia*—from the moon, knowledge—because it was the three astronauts' intention to increase man's knowledge through exploration of an ancient area of the moon known as Fra Mauro. Strewn over Fra Mauro, scientists believed, were boulders and rocky debris that may have come from deep within the moon and may, therefore, be fragments of the moon's original crust. Apollo 13, however, never reached Fra Mauro. It never made it to the moon. And there were moments, as tense and perilous as any in the short history of space flight, when it was feared that the three astronauts might never return to earth. What was to have been a voyage of exploration became a voyage of survival.

The trouble began on the night of April 13, 1970, as Apollo 13 neared the moon. The three astronauts had just completed a leisurely television show in which they demonstrated how to enter the Lunar Module. The commander was James A. Lovell Jr., the 42-year-old Navy captain who had logged more hours in space (572 hours before Apollo 13) than any other man. One of Lovell's crewmen was Fred W. Haise Jr., the 36-year-old Lunar Module pilot who was supposed to walk on the moon with Lovell. Haise, a former Marine pilot, was a civilian making his first flight in space. The third man, the Command Module pilot, was John L. Swigert Jr., another civilian and space rookie—and also a late-hour substitute on the mission. Swigert, 38 years old, was named to the crew the day before launching, replacing Thomas K. Mattingly II, who had been exposed to German measles and was thought to be coming down with the disease. But Swigert was well trained as a back-up pilot, and Apollo 13's flight had gone smoothly for two and a half days—until the three men were 205,000 miles out from earth.

Then there was a loud bang.

Although they did not know it until the mission was almost over, an explosion had blown out practically one entire side of the cylindrical Service Module, the engine room that rode behind the cone-shaped Command Module. One of the oxygen tanks had exploded.

Almost immediately an alarm light in front of the astronauts showed a drop in voltage on half their main electrical system. Seeing this, Swigert called out to Mission Control, "Hey, we've got a problem here!"

"Say again, please," Mission Control asked for clarification.

Lovell came on the circuit. His voice was matter-of-fact. "Houston," he said, "we've had a problem. We've had a main B-bus interval."

At that point, Haise was emerging from the tunnel leading into the LM. As he pulled his weightless body into the Command Module seat, his eye caught the instrument panel. The voltage in half of the electrical system had dropped to zero.

Something catastrophic had obviously happened. Mission Control tensed. Reporters in the nearby newsroom, who had been making their dinner plans, stopped, listened, and went to their telephones. "We had a pretty large bang," they heard Haise say over the radio, as they warned their editors to expect a whole new story.

But what *had* happened? At first a meteorite impact was suspected, but a rise in oxygen pressure just before the rupture made it more likely that the problem was of internal origin. Looking back toward the Service Module, Lovell could see a blizzard of particles flying out, presumably from one or more ruptured tanks. "It looks to me," Lovell reported, "that we're venting something out into space. . . . It's a gas of some sort."

Apollo 13 kept venting, and the venting had the effect of random rocket firings. The spaceship became unsteady, dipping its nose and rolling. Worst of all, despite desperate measures suggested by Mission Control, nothing would halt the drop in oxygen pressure.

"I don't like to say this," Seymour Liebergot, the controller in charge of electrical, environmental and communications (EECOM) systems, finally said, "but I think we've lost a fuel cell."

The Service Module contained tanks of liquid oxygen and liquid hydrogen and three fuel cells. By combining hydrogen and oxygen, the fuel cells generated electricity and made water. If one fuel cell should shut down, it could not be re-started; it would mean that the astronauts could still get back to earth, but all plans for a moon landing would have to be abandoned.

Then Haise reported that two of the three fuel cells were dead. One oxygen tank was empty and the other was losing pressure fast—evidently it had been ruptured by the explosion in the first tank. With all pressure gone, the last power-generating fuel cell would also go dead.

"It's slowly going to zero," Mission Control advised the astronauts, referring to the remaining oxygen tank, "and we are starting to think about the LM lifeboat."

"Yes," replied Swigert, "that's something we're thinking about, too."

Apollo 13 had no other choice. A lunar landing was impossible. The problem now was to get the men safely back to earth. With the Service Module's fuel cells dead, the astronauts would have to rely on the limited battery electricity, water and oxygen of the attached Lunar Module. So, like mariners abandoning ship, Lovell and Haise retreated through the darkened tunnel leading to the Command Module, *Odyssey*, and occupied the Lunar Module, *Aquarius*.

Swigert remained in *Odyssey*. Two things had to be done in a hurry. Enough oxygen had to be saved from the Service Module to supply the Command Module during re-entry into the earth's atmosphere—assuming they could get back to earth—and the gyros in the navigation system had to be kept going until the navigation equipment of the LM could be powered up.

Though it was little comfort at the time, the situation could have been worse. If the accident had to happen, it had occurred when the astronauts could still make such a retreat to the LM. Had the Service Module become disabled later, either during the lunar landing or afterward, the astronauts would have been without their lifeboat. In the first case, the LM would be on the moon, and even if it could rejoin the Command Module it would have already used up nearly all of its rocket power and most of its oxygen and electricity. In the latter case, the LM would have already been discarded. The astronauts would have been doomed. But for the moment they were too busy to reflect on how dire their condition might have been.

With only minutes remaining, the astronauts fed oxygen into a reserve tank on the Command Module and hooked up emergency batteries to the gyros. This kept them alive until the LM navigation system warmed up. That done, Swigert promptly switched off the battery power, which had to be conserved for reentry. *Odyssey* was a dead craft.

Using the LM as a lifeboat had been rehearsed many times on the ground, but this was the real thing, and flight controllers and the astronauts knew they had little margin for error or delay. They had no chance at all if anything should now happen to the LM's vital systems. This was very much on the minds of space agency officials when they finally emerged from the control room a few hours after the explosion. Christopher C. Kraft, who had served as flight director or mission executive on all of the nation's manned spaceflights, said that this was "as serious a situation as we have ever had in manned spaceflight."

There were still some crucial decisions to be made. At that point in the flight, the spaceship was too far from earth to turn around in midcourse. It was, in effect, falling toward the moon, and it would have required far more rocket power than was available to defy the moon's gravity and head homeward immediately. Instead, it was decided, the astronauts would ride around the moon, allowing lunar gravity, in a crack-the-whip manner, to throw the crippled vehicle back in the general direction of the earth. The general strategy for the return trip was decided upon early the next morning.

The first step was to fire the LM rocket briefly so as to push the combined spaceship into a trajectory that, after looping the moon, would return Apollo 13 on a more precise course to earth. Ground controllers rejected the idea of using the Service Module rocket, for it might cause further damage to *Odyssey.*

Aligning *Aquarius* for the rocket firing turned out to be a difficult task. Normally, all that is required is for an astronaut to take star sightings and feed the data into the guidance computer. But the spaceship was enveloped in a swirl of frothy flakes generated by the venting gas and floating debris from the explosion. "Looks like I'm right in the middle of the Milky Way," Haise remarked. With sunlight reflected off the particles, it was impossible for the astronauts to find their guiding stars.

To overcome the problem, Mission Control figured out a way to align Apollo 13 by bringing the sun squarely into one of the spacecraft windows. The alignment was rehearsed several times on ground simulators, and then on Apollo 13. It worked. And so, with confidence, the LM rocket was fired for 30.7 seconds to alter Apollo 13's course so that it would miss the moon by 136 miles and swing back toward earth.

As Apollo 13 prepared to pass around the moon, Mission Control weighed several alternatives for speeding up the return trip. There was still concern that the LM's supply of consumables —oxygen, electricity and water—might not be sufficient. With that in mind, some flight controllers suggested firing the Service Module's rocket behind the moon with enough force to bring Apollo 13 back in 38 hours. Too risky, Mission Control decided. Who could predict what would happen—another explosion, possibly—when the rocket ignited? Another suggestion was to jettison the Service Module then and there, lightening Apollo 13's load and making a 40-hour return possible with the smaller LM rocket. This was ruled out, however, because it would so deplete the LM's rocket fuel that none would be left to make any necessary midcourse corrections. Moreover, the loss of the Service Module would expose the Command Module's heat shield to the possibly damaging ultraviolet radiations and temperature extremes of space. Without a sound heat shield, it would be impossible for the astronauts to survive the fiery heat of re-entry.

One after another, new flight plans were suggested, analyzed and rejected. Finally, some twelve hours after the explosion, Mission Control had made its decision and radioed new instructions to Apollo 13. The astronauts were to go ahead and loop the moon and then fire the LM rocket again to send their spaceship—all of it, the Service Module, the Command Module and the Lunar Module—on a faster and more accurate course toward earth. They would speed up, but they would not use up all their fuel reserves in one all-out firing.

At 9:41 P.M., after rounding the moon nearly 24 hours after the explosion, the rocket was fired 4½ minutes and Apollo 13 headed toward a splashdown three days later. It was then a race between time and the LM's dwindling reserves of water, oxygen and electricity. There were moments, Lovell confessed later, when the astronauts doubted that they would return alive.

Lifeboats at sea are not known for comfort, and *Aquarius* was no better. The men became fatigued, cold and sometimes irritable. Twice the weary astronauts inadvertently used the wrong controls and were told to use stimulant pills to get them through the last hours.

The cold was a particular problem. Without electricity for the heaters in *Odyssey*, the temperatures dropped to as low as 38 degrees Fahrenheit, and the astronauts bundled up in extra pairs of underwear when they tried to sleep. But besides the discomfort, the lack of heat worried the astronauts. They feared that some of the instruments needed for re-entry would freeze beyond recovery. When possible, therefore, the spacecraft was put into a "barbecue mode" of rotation so that the sun would uniformly heat all sides. But the gas venting kept twisting and tossing the vehicle.

Another problem called for considerable Yankee ingenuity—"shade tree engineering," Mission Control called it. When carbon dioxide rose to dangerous levels inside the spaceship, the astronauts had to assemble a "homemade" air purification system with the step-by-step guidance of ground controllers.

Ordinarily, the Apollo spaceship is amply equipped to cleanse the air of carbon dioxide by filtering it through a canister containing lithium hydroxide. But, with the Command Module powered down, the entire job was thrown to the smaller Lunar Module, which was equipped with enough lithium hydroxide only for the short time two men would have been on the moon. Moreover, it was discovered that the filtering canisters in the Command Module were not interchangeable with those in the LM. So the astronauts took spacesuit hoses, friction tape and other odd pieces of equipment and devised a way to let the Lunar Module's fans blow the spacecraft's air through the Command Module's cleansing system. The astronauts even stuffed a sock into the connection to make sure it worked. Soon carbon dioxide ceased to be a problem.

Between improvisations, the astronauts caught some naps and made two midcourse corrections with the LM rocket. But Apollo 13 still had some critical hours ahead of it. Before the Command Module could re-enter the atmosphere, the astronauts had to turn on its power after days of inactivity, stabilize the spaceship, cast off the Lunar Module and then jettison the damaged Service Module. The exact sequence of maneuvers was plotted down to the second by Eugene Kranz and a special team of flight controllers.

The world waited anxiously on that Friday, April 17, 1970. The USS *Iwo Jima* was standing by in the South Pacific, waiting for splashdown. Thirteen nations, including the Soviet Union, had offered ships or planes to help in the rescue operation, should Apollo 13 splash down far off target. Prayers were said in the Vatican by Pope Paul, at the Wailing Wall in Jerusalem, and at houses of worship all over the world. Even those who had professed loudly during Apollo 12 that they were bored with space found themselves watching television hour after hour like millions of others, watching and listening in their offices and homes, in stores and bars and train stations.

All through the night before splashdown Lovell, Haise and Swigert hardly slept. They were tense and cold and also busy rehearsing procedures for their final maneuvers. Like the whole flight plan, those maneuvers had been rewritten as a result of the accident.

Just before re-entry, Lovell, in *Aquarius*, fired up four 100-pound LM thruster jets to push the complete spaceship forward. Then Swigert, at the controls of the reactivated *Odyssey*, fired off explosive bolts and severed the connection with the Service Module. After the separation, Lovell backed the rest of their ship away from the Service Module with another rocket firing. This push-pull maneuver put the men a safe distance from the Service Module.

Next, Swigert turned on electricity in the Command Module's guidance system. The surge of power put the astronauts' minds at rest. The electronics had survived the cold. Lovell and Haise then joined Swigert in the Command Module, closed the hatches and cut the link with their lifeboat, *Aquarius*. Like a toy balloon that is suddenly released, *Aquarius* moved away from *Odyssey*, propelled by the oxygen escaping from the end of the tunnel.

"LM jettisoned," one of the Apollo 13 astronauts announced.

"OK," Mission Control radioed back. "Farewell, *Aquarius*, and we thank you."

That was the parting tribute from Mission Control to the

tumbling Lunar Module that had saved the lives of the three men of Apollo 13. The rest of the flight, the re-entry into the atmosphere and the parachute-assisted splashdown, was routine and safe. After splashdown, President Nixon flew to meet the astronauts, and the world caught its breath.

Apollo 13 will not be remembered for its short circuits and defective switches. Apollo 13 may have failed in its immediate mission, but it gave the world a sharper appreciation of the sheer audacity of man's drive to reach the moon. It took Apollo 13's near-disaster to give perspective to Apollo 11's initial triumph.

APOLLO 14: COMEBACK FLIGHT

It was nine months before astronauts and their machines were again ready to fly to the moon and attempt man's third landing. Late in January 1971, the countdown for Apollo 14 began in an atmosphere of unusual anxiety. Success of a mission never seemed of greater importance to its participants; the specter of another failure never seemed so ominous. The explosion on Apollo 13 was very much on the minds of the engineers, astronauts and scientists of Apollo 14 during the countdown at Cape Kennedy.

The engineers looked to Apollo 14 to demonstrate that they had eliminated the workmanship flaws responsible for Apollo 13's troubles. In the previous nine months, they had made a dozen changes in the spaceship for safety's sake. These modifications included the addition of a third oxygen tank in the Service Module, isolated from the two regular tanks; installation of an extra, high-capacity battery for emergency power; and redesigning the oxygen tank and enclosing tank wiring in metal conduits.

The astronauts were especially eager for a successful nine-day mission to erase the "stigma," as they put it, of the previous failure. That stigma had been partly responsible, along with new budget reductions, for the elimination of two Apollo flights that had been planned for later in the program. Another failure might revive arguments that manned spaceflights were unjustifiably risky and expensive, thus leading possibly to further Apollo cancellations. "If Apollo 14 doesn't go well," Walter C. Kapryan, the new launching director, said, "we may not have a future at all."

With so few Apollos left and so much still to be learned about the moon, the scientists could hardly contain their excitement at the prospect of Apollo 14 landing in the midst of rocks that could be nearly as old as the solar system—about 4.6 billion years—and a billion years older than most of the fragments gathered on the lunar plains by Apollos 11 and 12. For Apollo 14's landing target was the same Fra Mauro highlands selected for Apollo 13. Fra Mauro is situated on the eastern shore of the Ocean of Storms, near the equator on the left side of the moon's face as seen from earth.

If Apollo 14 had all the makings of a comeback flight for the project, it also represented a personal comeback for the crew's commander, Alan B. Shepard Jr. At the age of 47, when most men get winded running for a bus, Shepard was in remarkably good physical condition and ready to pick up where he left off a decade earlier when he became America's first man in space.

With Shepard on Apollo 14 were two space rookies. Edgar D. Mitchell was a 40-year-old Navy commander who held a doctorate in aeronautics and astronautics from the Massachusetts Institute of Technology; he was the LM pilot who would go down to the moon with Shepard. Stuart A. Roosa was a 37-year-old Air Force major and test pilot; he was the Command Module pilot, the man who would stay with the mother ship in lunar orbit while the other two men landed on the moon.

As the three astronauts set out for the moon on January 31,

the pre-flight anxieties seemed all too justified. About three hours after lift-off, shortly after Apollo 14 rocketed out of low earth orbit, the first of several brief but potentially serious problems arose.

When Roosa attempted to steer the nose of the command ship, *Kitty Hawk,* into the docking ring of the LM, *Antares,* the latches would not catch. The two vehicles had to link up so that the LM could be pulled from its attachment to the Saturn 5's third stage. Roosa made five futile attempts. Each time the latches failed Roosa would back the command ship away, discuss the problem with Mission Control and then try again. Finally, on the sixth try, Roosa was successful. If he had not been, all plans for Apollo 14's lunar landing would have been abandoned.

Even though the astronauts and ground engineers could never determine what went wrong, Mission Control cleared Apollo 14 to go into lunar orbit on February 4 and to make the landing attempt the next morning. If the docking problem recurred when the LM returned from the moon to rendezvous with the command ship, flight directors said, Shepard and Mitchell could always open their hatch and "walk" a short distance across the void of space to rejoin Roosa.

Early on the morning of February 5, Shepard and Mitchell entered their landing craft. After the two ships separated, Shepard and Mitchell were preparing to fire the descent rocket for the landing when a second mysterious problem threatened the mission.

Flight controllers scanning the radioed data from *Antares* discovered that the landing craft's abort switch was sending a false signal to the craft's main computer. Normally, the switch would be activated only if the astronauts wanted to abort, or break off, the lunar landing attempt because of some trouble. The misbehaving switch did not endanger the crew, but it could prevent a landing if it sent a false signal after the descent engine started firing. Something had to be done, and done quickly. Guidance experts at M.I.T., Cape Kennedy and the Manned Spacecraft Center conferred by telephone and decided on a way to circumvent the switch. In less than an hour they wrote a new set of computer instructions, checked them out in simulators, and then had the astronauts insert the new "program" into the guidance computer just moments before starting the final descent to the moon.

The final descent from an altitude of 45,000 feet took 12 minutes 46 seconds, and used up all but a minute of the rocket fuel. "Right on the landing site," Shepard reported after hovering for a short time and then touching down at 4:18 A.M.

When the two men were preparing for their first walk out on that undulating terrain, they encountered a communications problem. Mission Control was receiving data but no voices from the astronauts through their backpack transmitters. It was apparently only a switching problem in the spacecraft, a circuit breaker left open unintentionally. But it was enough to delay the walk about 50 minutes.

At 9:49 A.M., the astronauts opened the hatch of *Antares* and began the first of two moon walks—the first one running 4 hours 40 minutes and the second, 4 hours 39 minutes.

On the first walk, the astronauts concentrated on establishing the ALSEP (Apollo Lunar Surface Experiments Package) near the landing craft. The Apollo 12 ALSEP was still operating after more than a year, and a comparable longevity for the Apollo 14 package was expected. Mitchell also set out three geophones, which were sensitive to vibrations, and then provided the vibrations with a staff containing small explosive charges. Every 15 feet, Mitchell pressed the "thumper" against the lunar surface and fired off a charge. Seismic readings, monitored on earth, revealed the structure of the topsoil in that area as being a 50-foot layer of loose material overlying what was thought to be rock or highly compacted material.

Early the next morning, February 6, Shepard and Mitchell went back outside and began the longest and most arduous moon hike yet undertaken. Their goal was the rim of Cone Crater, a 400-foot-high mound that stood several thousand feet away from *Antares*. To haul tools and cameras for their "field trip," the astronauts had a rickshaw-like, two-wheeled cart that they pulled across the rocky surface.

On their walk Shepard and Mitchell observed some fairly fresh craters, a lot of tiny pebbles and, to the delight of scientists, a few white rocks unlike anything seen by Apollo 11 and 12 astronauts.

"You know," Shepard said after about two hours of hiking, "we haven't reached the rim yet."

Consulting his map and surveying the horizon, Shepard thought he saw the rim of Cone Crater, but it was by his estimate, a good 30-minute hike away. After considerable discussion between themselves and with Mission Control, the astronauts decided against trying to reach Cone Crater and concentrated instead on collecting samples in the boulder field where they were standing. They chipped off a fragment from a large "almost white" boulder. Geologists at Mission Control, though disappointed by the failure to reach Cone Crater, felt sure the astronauts had accomplished what they set out to do: Collect some rocks that may have been gouged from deep within the moon and, consequently, were remnants of the original lunar crust.

After the astronauts returned to their landing craft and rested, they ended their 33½-hour visit to the moon. *Antares* rocketed off the surface at 1:49 P.M. and in two hours rejoined the command ship, *Kitty Hawk*. The link-up between the two ships produced a great sigh of relief in Mission Control; for whatever the docking problem had been on the first day of the flight, it had not recurred. The three-day homeward flight was then under way, and it was a flawless journey.

Apollo 14, returning with 96 pounds of lunar rock and leaving a smoothly operating scientific station at Fra Mauro, came to a successful conclusion with a pinpoint splashdown in the Pacific Ocean on February 9.

CHAPTER 16

Beyond
Apollo

In the decade of Apollo, with the voyages to the moon, man made at least two profound discoveries. He learned that he could fly into space, leaving his native planet for the first time and reaching into another world, the moon. He also discovered Earth. He saw Earth whole for the first time and found it, as he knew it must be but had never quite appreciated it, a small and cloud-streaked blue spaceship on which all mankind depends for its precarious existence.

EXPLORING THE UNFAMILIAR

In the coming years, man expects to extend his reach to the very edge of the solar system. He will not go there himself—

not yet. But his cameras and electronic sensors, like remote eyes and ears, will go on spaceships headed in toward Venus and Mercury and out toward Mars, Jupiter, Saturn, Uranus, Neptune and Pluto.

There will be unmanned spacecraft orbiting Mars to map its surface and eventually to land there and search for any possible life. There will, in time, be men making that long journey to Mars. But before that, there will be the spacecraft flying past Venus and on to take the first photographs and close-up measurements of Mercury. Jupiter, the largest of the sun's planets, will be having visitors. These unmanned spacecraft will be flying by for a close look at that mysterious red spot on Jupiter, the unusually high energy outputs, the surrounding radiations, and the 12 satellites. They will also be flying by on their way to the outer planets, using Jupiter's tremendous mass for a "gravity-assist" to gather the energy necessary to reach Saturn and Pluto or Uranus and Neptune. In the late Seventies, the orbits of the outer planets will begin lining up in such a way that will not happen again for 179 more years. The alignment will present scientists with a rare opportunity to fly an unmanned spacecraft by all five planets over a period of about ten to twelve years, an achievement that would otherwise take some 30 years with present rocket technology.

While planetary exploration should be the most exciting of the immediate post-Apollo goals, the United States and the Soviet Union are both expected to place considerable emphasis on manned explorations of the near-earth regions of space. After Apollo, American astronauts are planning to test an experimental space station, called Skylab, for periods of 28 and 56 days each. Within a decade, Americans could be flying into and back from space in a new type of vehicle that is as much airplane as spacecraft. In fact, its planners are calling it an aerospaceplane.

Such a vehicle, designed to shuttle men and satellites and supplies to and from earth orbit, would leave earth like a rocket. Its manned orbital craft would rendezvous with a space station or some satellite in need of resupply, refueling or repair. After completing its work, or the transfer of crews, the shuttle would return to earth. Because of its aerodynamic shape it would be capable of gliding in to a landing on any jet airport. After a few weeks for inspections and refueling, it could be ready to go back into space. The shuttle and its planned orbit-to-orbit counterpart, the space tug, are considered by American space planners to be the type of vehicles, reusable and relatively inexpensive to operate, that would make it possible to send more amd more people into space. Such vehicles would also be instrumental in manned expeditions to Mars and in establishing and maintaining semi-permanent outposts on the moon.

APOLLO 15: "EXPLORATION AT ITS GREATEST"

Before the Apollo Project drew to its close, there was a significant change in the emphasis of the missions to the moon. The earlier journeys had been demonstrations of an engineering capability; reaching the moon was the primary goal. But the later flights concentrated on science and discovery.

For this purpose the Command Module and the Lunar Module were modified. Oxygen and hydrogen tanks were added to extend the mission time. A bay in the Service Module, the rear compartment of the Command Module, was outfitted with cameras and scientific instruments for investigations from lunar orbit. The Lunar Module was equipped with more water, oxygen, battery power and propellants for a 72-hour stay on the moon. (Armstrong and Aldrin had stayed less than 22 hours.) And the astronauts' space suits were also modified to increase the time they could spend outside the Lunar Module from $4\frac{1}{2}$ hours to $7\frac{1}{2}$ hours on each excursion.

The first of these science-oriented flights was Apollo 15. On July 26, 1971, Colonel David R. Scott, Lieutenant Colonel James B. Irwin, and Major Alfred M. Worden Jr., all Air Force pilots, embarked on their journey from Cape Kennedy. Four days later, Scott and Irwin piloted their Lunar Module, the *Falcon*, to a landing in the most awesome terrain yet explored on the moon.

They landed in a small lunar plain called *Palus Putredinis*, the Latin name for Marsh of Decay. What made it such a spectacular place were the plain's surroundings. Nearby was Hadley Rille, a meandering gorge a mile wide and, in places, 1200 feet deep. Much of the cratered plain was enclosed by the towering Apennine Mountains. Some of the rounded peaks rose 15,000 feet above the flatlands.

"As I stand out here in the wonders of the unknown at Hadley," Scott, the mission commander, said, "I sort of realize there is a fundamental truth to our nature. Man must explore. And this is exploration at its greatest."

Scott and Irwin did more exploring than the three previous moon-landing crews combined. In three excursions outside *Falcon*, they covered 17½ miles in a total of 18½ hours. They were able to go such great distances, to the rim of the gorge and to the slopes of the mountains, because of an unusual vehicle—the lunar rover.

The rover, sometimes called the moon buggy, was hauled to the moon in a compartment in the lower half of the Lunar Module. It had four hollow, wire-mesh wheels designed to withstand the jolts and bumps of jagged rocks. It ran on electricity from two large storage batteries, and had a top speed of 10 miles an hour.

On their first drive, Scott and Irwin went to the rim of Hadley Rille and the slopes of the Apennines. At a number of stops, they switched on the color television camera mounted on the front of the lunar rover. The camera was focused and pointed by remote control from Mission Control in Houston.

Thus, as the astronauts walked out from the rover, the world could "accompany" them as they collected rocks and examined their strange surroundings. People on earth could see and hear Scott as he contemplated a glass-speckled rock standing alone. "Imagine," Scott reflected, "it's been here since before creatures roamed the sea or land."

On the second excursion, the astronauts drove a short way up a gentle mountain slope. They discovered there a crystalline rock that became known as the "Genesis Rock." The rock was of the type believed to have been common in the earliest lunar crust. This led an excited David Scott to radio to Mission Control, "I think we got what we came for." However, later analysis showed the rock to be 4.1 billion years old. That makes it a half-billion years younger than the moon itself.

When Scott and Irwin drove to Hadley Rille on their final excursion, they picked up a sample from exposed bedrock. They also reported that the walls of the canyon were marked with a distinct layering pattern. This suggested that many separate events, lava flows and scattering of fresh debris, shaped the lunar surface over the ages—just as the layered walls of the Grand Canyon reveal much of earth's evolutionary geology.

Then, on August 2, after nearly 67 hours on the moon, *Falcon* blasted away from the plain of Hadley. The television camera on the rover, which was left behind, telecast the lift-off. On the airless moon, there were no great flames in the rocket's exhaust. The colorful flames at Cape Kennedy depend on oxygen in the atmosphere. But the force of the lunar lift-off scattered dust and ripped metal particles from the Lunar Module's landing base. Because of the one-sixth gravity and the vehicle's light weight, the Lunar Module's getaway was quick, almost sudden, in contrast to the slow, struggling launches from earth.

The Apollo 15 astronauts remained in lunar orbit for two more days. This allowed Worden to complete the scientific and photographic work he had been doing while Scott and Irwin were on the moon.

Instruments in the Service Module recorded high concentrations of aluminum in the lunar highlands and low concentrations in the plains. This was one more piece of evidence suggesting the great difference between the two basic features on the moon. A magnetometer detected a very weak lunar magnetic field. This surprised scientists, who had thought there was no field at all.

Worden reported seeing small conical mounds near the Sea of Serenity. They appeared to be dead volcanic craters. This indicated that the moon once had a hot interior and was volcanically active. Then, before Apollo 15 left lunar orbit, Worden launched a 78½-pound scientific satellite that was to gather data from lunar orbit for nearly a year.

On August 7, Apollo 15 splashed down in the Pacific Ocean. One of the three parachutes collapsed soon after it unfurled, making the splashdown somewhat harder than usual. But this in no way detracted from the many accomplishments of Apollo 15.

APOLLO 16: TO THE MOUNTAINS OF THE MOON

No matter how many times you see and hear and feel an Apollo launching, it never fails to send a tingling shiver racing up your spine. The launching of Apollo 16 on April 16, 1972 was no different.

Orange flames spread from the base of the mammoth Saturn 5 rocket. The 36-story moonship rose ponderously off the launching pad. The earth shook for miles around, and thunderclaps of sound rolled across the sandy plain. The sky was so clear and blue that the rocket's fiery exhaust could be seen with the unaided eye for several minutes, first as a glowing ball of flame, then as a red arrow with a vapor trail, and finally as a tiny star over the Atlantic Ocean.

Captain John W. Young and Lieutenant Commander Thomas K. Mattingly II of the Navy and Lieutenant Colonel Charles M. Duke Jr. of the Air Force were on their way to the moon. It was the next-to-last mission in the Apollo series of moon exploration.

There were many times when the three astronauts wondered if fate was against them. For Apollo 16 encountered a rash of ir- ritating malfunctions. Some insulation paint peeled off the lunar module. A false computer signal temporarily locked the space- craft's navigation alignment system. An antenna stuck in one position. Nevertheless, Apollo 16 continued and reached lunar orbit. Young, the mission commander, cried out: "Boy, this has got to be the neatest way to make a living anybody's ever in- vented."

Then came a potentially more serious malfunction. After Young and Duke had moved into the Lunar Module and cast off from the command ship, Mattingly reported trouble with the Com- mand Module's secondary guidance system. It was causing slight but disturbing oscillations in the main rocket engine.

For a few anxious hours, Mission Control weighed the possi- bility that Apollo 16 might have to leave lunar orbit and return to earth without a landing. Although the situation was not as life- threatening as the Apollo 13 accident, concern mounted. It was a question of crew safety. If more serious trouble should develop, it might be necessary for the Lunar Module, still fully fueled, to provide the rocket power for the emergency return.

But an analysis by ground engineers reassured Mission Control that there was a "very large safety factor" in proceeding with the landing. Accordingly, Young and Duke steered the Lunar Module, *Orion,* to a delayed but successful landing on April 20.

It was man's first visit to the lunar highlands. Apollo 15 had only touched the fringes of the mountains. Now Apollo 16 touched down in one of the highest regions on the front face of the moon. Their landing site was a rolling, boulder-strewn plateau surrounded by mountains and craters. The site, in the southeastern quarter of the moon, was known as Descartes, after a nearby crater.

Young and Duke spent a record 71 hours on the moon, including 21½ hours outside *Orion* on three separate EVA's (extravehicular activity). Like the Apollo 15 explorers, they used a lunar rover to extend their range of work and discovery.

What they found surprised many scientists. Before Apollo 16, lunar geologists thought the Descartes area had been formed from a series of lava flows from volcanic eruptions early in the moon's history. And they assumed that the surface had lain relatively undisturbed since the time of the lava flows. They hoped so, because it would give them proof that vulcanism, as well as meteorite bombardment, had helped to shape the lunar surface.

If this were true, the two astronauts expected to find many crystalline rocks, the type formed when lava cools off and hardens. But they found mostly breccias, which are rocks composed of other rock fragments welded together by heat. Most breccias on the moon are thought to have resulted from meteorite impacts rather than from volcanic activity.

It was still possible that the Descartes area was originally a lava flow. But much had happened since then to plow up the surface. Young described what he saw as "craters on top of craters on top of craters."

Once again, the moon had turned out to be a more complex place than scientists had supposed. Apollo 17, the last flight in the Apollo series, revealed still more complexities.

APOLLO 17

Apollo 17 was not just another flight to the moon. It was the last flight to the moon of the Apollo series. It was the culmination of all that had gone before—the Kennedy challenge and the Apollo 1 fire, Walter Schirra and Apollo 7, Frank Borman and Apollo 8, Neil Armstrong and Apollo 11 and Tranquility Base. After an expenditure of $25 billion over eleven years, after nine flights to the environs of the moon and six landings, the great American enterprise known as Apollo came to an end with Apollo 17 in late 1972.

The finale was almost perfect. There were surprisingly few equipment malfunctions. The ambitious plan for the 12½-day mission was followed almost to the letter. Scientists received a wealth of the raw material of lunar science: a record 249 pounds of rocks and soil, 3,000 photographs of the surface, miles of magnetic tapes containing data of the moon's physical structure.

The astronauts of Apollo 17 were Captain Eugene A. Cernan of the Navy, Commander Ronald E. Evans of the Navy and Dr. Harrison H. Schmitt, a geologist and the first scientist to be assigned to an American space mission.

Their flight to the moon, the last for years to come, started in a spectacular manner with the first nighttime launching of American astronauts. It had to be that way if Apollo 17 was to land at the right place at the right time.

In the early morning hours of December 7, 1972, the fiery exhaust of the Saturn 5 turned the dark night into blinding day at Cape Kennedy. For those spectators who failed to wear dark glasses the sudden invasion of their night-dilated eyes by the brilliance left transient spots on their retinas.

Three days later, on December 10, the Apollo 17 spaceship rocketed into an orbit of the moon. Leaving Evans to pilot the command ship America in orbit, Cernan and Schmitt boarded the lunar module Challenger and cast off on December 11 for the landing on the moon.

"The Challenger has landed," a jubilant Cernan radioed to Mission Control. "We is here. Man, we is here!"

The Challenger had landed among the boulders and craters of a narrow valley near the southeast rim of the Sea of Serenity, the easternmost landing site of an Apollo crew. To the north rose the steep walls of a 5,000-foot mountain. To the south stood a 7,000-foot mountain with rock slides at its base. Over the valley floor was scattered a dark dusty covering, perhaps young volcanic ash. The astronauts called the site Taurus-Littrow, after the nearby Taurus Mountains and the Littrow Crater.

Within four hours of the landing, Cernan and Schmitt began the first of three excursions outside their landing craft. They set up a science station. The instruments were designed to measure the flow of heat from the lunar interior, to determine variations in gravity, to detect traces of lunar gases, to listen to internal shock waves from explosive charges and to observe impacts of micrometeorites.

On their second excursion, on December 12, the two astronauts came upon the biggest scientific surprise of the mission. It was at the crater they called Shorty. When Schmitt walked near the rim, he saw what appeared to be orange and red soil, something he said he never expected to find on the moon.

His conversation with Cernan, overheard by Mission Control, was a rare and exciting moment in discovery.

Schmitt: "There is orange soil."
Cernan: "Well, don't move it till I see it."
Schmitt: "I stirred it with my foot."
Cernan: "Hey, it is. I can see it from here."
Schmitt: "It's orange."
Cernan: "Wait a minute, let me put my (sun) visor up. It's still orange."

Schmitt: "Sure is. Crazy. Orange."

Cernan: "He's not going out of his wits, it really is."

Whereupon, scientists at Mission Control jumped closer to the closed-circuit television sets. The lunar rover's color television camera, remotely operated from Mission Control, was focusing in on the soil at Shorty. The scientists could see for themselves the orange soil. One of them, Dr. Robin Brett of the Manned Spacecraft Center, called the discovery "one of the most important finds in Apollo geology."

After further examination on the moon, Schmitt said, "If there ever was something that looked like a fumarole alteration, this is it."

On earth, a fumarole is a vent through which gases have escaped from the interior. It is considered one of the last stages of activity after a volcanic eruption. Around such a vent the gases create oxides, or rust, through the chemical reaction between the minerals and oxygen and water vapor. Does this also occur on the moon? This was one of the most intriguing questions raised by Apollo 17.

The third and final excursion on December 13, saw the two astronauts drive the lunar rover to the foot of the north mountain wall. They cast eight-foot shadows as they examined the cracks, blue-green crystals and glassy veins of two huge boulders that had come to rest there after tumbling down the steep slope thousands, perhaps millions of years ago.

Working around the boulders, chipping off fragments and collecting soil, Schmitt remarked, "I feel like a kid playing in a sandbox."

Back at the lunar module, ending the last moon walk of Apollo, Cernan and Schmitt unveiled a plaque attached to one of the four legs of the vehicle. In words reminiscent of the plaque left by the first men to walk on the moon, the Apollo 17 plaque read:

> Here man completed his first
> Explorations of the moon
> December 1972, A.D.
> May the spirit of peace in which we came
> Be reflected in the lives of all mankind.

Altogether, Cernan and Schmitt spent a record 23 hours and 12 minutes out on the surface of the moon over a period of more than three days. Then, on December 14, Challenger blasted off the surface, and Cernan and Schmitt rejoined Evans in the orbiting command ship.

Splashdown for Apollo 17, and for the Apollo Project, came December 19 in the Pacific Ocean south of American Samoa. It was a bull's-eye landing near the U.S.S. *Ticonderoga,* the aircraft carrier that served as the astronauts' recovery ship. It was the ending of Apollo 17, but the beginning of years of effort to extract the knowledge bound up in the rock samples, the photographs and the taped data.

On that occasion, President Nixon said, "The safe return of the command module America marks the end of one of the most significant chapters in the history of human endeavor."

René Descartes, the French mathematician and philosopher after whom Apollo 16's landing site was named, wrote: "There is nothing so far removed from us as to be beyond our reach, or so hidden that we cannot discover it."

Apollo has brought the moon within our reach. For years to come, as the rocks are analyzed and the data sifted, scientists will be discovering the moon and what it tells us about the origins of earth and the solar system.

Index

ABOUT THE AUTHOR

John Noble Wilford was born in Murray, Kentucky, and as the son of a Methodist minister, he had many hometowns in Kentucky and Tennessee. He received a B.S. in journalism at the University of Tennessee, an M.A. in political science at Syracuse University, and studied international politics and history at Columbia University as a Ford Foundation Fellow.

Mr. Wilford first came to New York City in 1956 to work as a reporter on *The Wall Street Journal.* After two years in the Army's Counter Intelligence Corps in West Germany, he again returned to New York City and *The Journal,* where he covered medicine and the drug industry.

In 1965, while a writer for the Science section of *Time Magazine,* Mr. Wilford began covering Apollo and the space program, and he continued his coverage of this program when he moved to *The New York Times* as its aerospace reporter.

The author lives in New York City with his wife Nancy and their daughter Nona.